Educating Language Minority Children

READ PERSPECTIVES

A publication of the READ Institute

EDITORS

Rosalie Pedalino Porter, Ed.D., *Editor*
Sean Fitzgerald, *Assistant Editor*
Jorge Amselle, *Production*

ACADEMIC REVIEW PANEL

Ralph E. Beals, Ph.D.
Professor of Economics
Amherst College

Robert E. Rossier, Ph.D.
Educational Consultant
Los Angeles, California

Kevin Clark
Clark Consulting Group
Stockton, California

Sandra Stotsky, Ed.D.
Deputy Commissioner
Massachusetts Department of Education

Jim Littleton
Former Program Director
Office for Civil Rights
U.S. Department of Education

Carol Whitten
Former Director
Office for Bilingual Education and Minority
Language Affairs U.S. Department of
Education

ADDITIONAL READERS

Norma McKenna and David T. Porter

READ INSTITUTE STAFF

Linda Chavez, Litt. D. (Honor), *President*
Jorge Amselle, *Executive Director*
Sean Fitzgerald, *Policy Analyst*

PRODUCTION

Sean Fitzgerald
Chrisite Weisenburg

Rosalie Pedalino Porter
editor

Educating Language Minority Children

Volume 6
READ Perspectives

Transaction Publishers
New Brunswick (U.S.A.) and London (U.K.)

ISSN: 1091-6822

ISBN: 0-7658-0669-X (paper)

Printed in the United States of America

Contents

INTRODUCTION

The current volume of *READ Perspectives*, which marks our sixth year of publication, represents a change from a biannual magazine to an annual serial publication within the Periodicals Consortium Group at Transaction Publishers, Rutgers University. Each volume will have a central theme, with our focus this year on "The Transitional State of Bilingual Education."

Charles L. Glenn of Boston University's School of Education and a long-time member of the READ Institute Academic Panel provided the seed that germinated into an impressive gathering of educational leaders whose presentations make up the major portion of this volume. Glenn wrote an essay for the Pioneer Institute in Boston, "Rethinking Bilingual Education," (*Agenda for Leadership*, 1998), in which he recommended a series of changes to Massachusetts' 1971 Transitional Bilingual Education law. Glenn's ideas for making essential, and long overdue, modifications to the legislation reflect the realities of the current status of immigrant education and build on the insights gained from a quarter century of research and practical experience. "Rethinking Bilingual Education" is reprinted in its entirety as the lead article in this volume.

It seems appropriate that the impetus for reasonable reform of bilingual education should come from the state that first institutionalized this teaching model by legislative mandate. Glenn's proposed changes in Massachusetts law—which could be sensibly applied anywhere in the nation—center on these main ideas: desegregate bilingual classrooms, introduce flexibility in program options for each school district, and monitor bilingual students' academic performance, holding them to the same high expectations as other students.

Illustrating the power of well-expressed ideas, Glenn's article also sparked the notion of organizing a conference to bring together a range of presentations covering disparate viewpoints on the issue of bilingual education reform. The READ Institute and the Pioneer Institute jointly sponsored a one-day conference titled "New Directions in Educating Language-Minority Children: An Agenda for the Future," held on October 30, 1998, at Boston University, with their

1

generous support. The papers presented at that conference consti-
tute the major portion of this volume. Three panels of educators,
researchers, and social scientists offered their views on what we
have learned from the recent research, what program practices look
promising, and what reforms are most urgently needed. These reports were delivered to an audience of 125 interested participants
from New England. Richard M. Estrada, editorial page editor for
the *Dallas Morning News*, delivered the keynote address.

One of the most gratifying expressions of appreciation for the conference came from a Boston educator of English language learners,
who was grateful for the broad range of ideas presented and the
civil tone of the discussions—two elements often missing from bilingual education gatherings. This participant remarked, "I came
hoping to have my prejudices confirmed, when in fact they were
rather challenged. The session went way beyond the usual war of
clichés into a bracing, stimulating, highly informative discussion....
It's what this issue needs—not more inflamed rhetoric ... but rea-
soned argument. That will carry the day in the end."

Panel One focused on a few examples of the latest reported research:
Diane August gave her views as co-author of the 1997 National
Research Council study *Improving Schooling for Language Minority
Children: A Research Agenda;* Christine H. Rossell delivered a critique
of the Thomas and Collier Study, "School Effectiveness for Language
Minority Students"; I reported on the findings of two research studies commissioned by the READ Institute on the El Paso Independent School District's programs for limited-English students, and
the last speaker on this panel, economist Mark Hugo Lopez of the
University of Maryland, reviewed his findings on the end product of
different education programs: the labor market earnings, ten years
after high school completion, of limited-English students who had
participated either in native language instruction programs or had
been educated in English language programs.

Panel Two presenters included Mary Cazabon, a leading proponent
of two-way bilingual programs, who reported on the outcomes in
language acquisition and academic achievement for public school
students in Cambridge, Massachusetts; Thomas J. Doluisio, superintendent of the Bethlehem (Pennsylvania) Area School District, who
described the change in his district from a Spanish bilingual pro-

gram for Puerto Rican, limited-English students, to an English Acquisition Program; and Boston University Professor Maria Estela Brisk, who contributed strong recommendations on how schools should be restructured to effectively educate language-minority students.

Panel Three featured different viewpoints on the need for legislative action. Charles L. Glenn summarized the main modifications he favors; Rep. Harold Lane, Chairman of the House Joint Committee on Education, Arts and Humanities in Massachusetts, spoke on the necessity of legislative reform, generally agreeing with the Glenn recommendations; and two school superintendents, Eugene Creedon of the Quincy Public Schools and Douglas Sears of the Chelsea Public Schools, discussed their ideas on needed reforms. The overriding consensus of the speakers was that bilingual education in Massachusetts must be improved, that liberalizing the state law from a one-size-fits-all teaching mandate to one that will allow for creative alternatives, *with a strong measure of accountability for bilingual students' academic progress*, would create genuinely better learning opportunities for bilingual children. Whether legislative change can occur in a timely fashion is not entirely clear, given the opposition of advocacy groups in this state.

To balance the Glenn essay on what legislative changes ought to be made in Massachusetts, the READ Institute commissioned a report on the early effects of legislative changes in California, whose citizens passed Proposition 227, the English for the Children Initiative, by 61 percent of the popular vote on June 2, 1998. Because California is the most populous state as well as having the highest proportion of immigrant families and limited-English students (1.2 million children, one of every five students in California schools), it is instructive to make a very preliminary assessment of the early effects of a new law that requires all English language learners to be placed in English immersion programs for one year, or for additional time, if necessary. There is a provision in the law for parents to request that their school continue to provide bilingual instruction for their children.

Kevin Clark, a program evaluator and teacher trainer with experience in hundreds of schools, conducted a survey of five representative California districts: Atwater, Ceres, Delano, Orange, and

Riverdale. In his report, he describes the measures taken by each district to implement the new law. Remarkably, in spite of differences in size, geography, and demographics, the districts observed took similar steps to establish new teaching guidelines, to explain the new approach to staff and parents to gain community support, and to put in place an evaluation process to monitor student achievement. Much more needs to be reported from California schools, and we look forward to substantially more data to be presented next year.

It would be fair to say that bilingual education as we have known it since 1968 is in a state of transition. With calm and reason and intelligence, its best feature—the recognition that limited-English students need special help—can be preserved and expanded. We must also acknowledge that no one teaching method is effective for all of these children—much can be improved by letting local initiatives and the creativity of individual teachers and schools flourish.

Rosalie Pedalino Porter, Editor
READ Perspectives

Rethinking BILINGUAL EDUCATION

Charles L. Glenn

Introduction

I will be arguing here that bilingual education programs that educate students separately have become a problem for school systems and for thousands of language-minority (LM) children, and
that integrated bilingual education is the solution. By "integrated
bilingual education" I mean making use of the language that children speak at home for support and supplemental instruction but
without segregating them in separate classes. To make this pedagogical change possible, fundamental reform of the legal and policy
framework within which language-minority children are schooled
is necessary.

Millions of children have passed through separate bilingual programs in the United States over the last thirty years. Some have
received a fine education in that way, but far too many have not.
Educating children who speak a language other than English at home
separately from other children until they can do school work at grade
level in both their home language and in English is an educational
experiment based on theories that have not held up in practice. It's
time we took another look. This article suggests changes in Massachusetts law and educational practice based on these decades of
experience. The article concludes with a series of recommendations
and Appendix A, which presents proposed revisions to the bilingual
education law, Chapter 71A.

This is not to say that teachers should neglect or fail to develop the
language skills children bring with them to school. Real reform of
bilingual education is not about suppressing languages or cultural
traditions; it is about equipping children to function well in our
schools and our society. Throwing children into a regular class with

This essay is reprinted, with permission of the author, from *Agenda for Leadership 1998*,
published by the Pioneer Institute for Public Policy Research in Boston.

5

a teacher not trained to meet their language development needs and without additional support along the way is both cruel and unwise. But so is "sheltering" them for years from the language and the curriculum they must eventually master. "Separate development" is not the way to go.

Choosing which pupils should participate in a language support program has been treated as the central question in efforts to scale back bilingual education in Massachusetts. Critics claim that pupils who could do perfectly well in regular classes are assigned to separate bilingual classes, often by misleading their parents with scare stories about the harm that would result from all-English instruction, and also that pupils are retained far too long after they should be assigned to a regular class. Those who defend the present program claim that parents are often misled by school officials into forgoing their right to a bilingual class, and that the great majority of pupils are "mainstreamed" after three years in bilingual education (though they do not count kindergarten as one of those years). Bilingual education advocates argue that learning academic subjects in the home language first leads students to greater academic success once they enter English-only classes.

It is obvious that academic skills do transfer from one language to another. A teenager who arrives here with well-developed skills from strong schooling in her homeland is likely to do well, after a few months of hard work and even struggle. But it does not follow that a child who was born here or has received inadequate schooling before immigrating should spend years acquiring academic skills in another language simply in order to transfer them to English. Someone who plays soccer will learn to play American football faster than someone else who has never played a sport, but that does not make it efficient to teach soccer first, if the goal is football. We should build on academic skills if a child already has them in another language, but we should not make developing new ones in that language a priority.

Is it valuable and enriching, other things being equal, for a pupil to learn and to learn through two languages? Of course! Should we make that possible? Yes! But should pupils acquiring a second language be kept separate from native speakers—pupils and even teachers—of that language for years and years? No!

WHY THE DEBATE IS CONFUSING

Discussion of bilingual education tends to become complicated, for three reasons:

1. The phrase is used to describe many different practices, from teaching language-minority (LM) children exclusively in their home language for years to teaching them in English with occasional help from their home language. For the purposes of this discussion, it will be best to use the phrase "separate bilingual program" to refer to the practice of assigning LM children to a separate class, whether taught in the home language or in English or in some mixture of both, for all of their formal instruction for a number of years.

There are other models also termed bilingual education. Children may be assigned to a regular class with pupils whose first language is English and pulled out for supplemental instruction and practice in English as a Second Language (ESL). Or they may be in such an integrated class with a teacher who has received special training in second-language development, and who modifies the instruction accordingly (perhaps with an aide for in-class help). Or the LM children may be in an integrated class in which both languages are used for instruction, with the goal that the children from homes where only English is spoken will also become bilingual: this is known as "two-way" bilingual education.[1] The difference between each of these cases and separate bilingual programs is not so much the manner in which instruction is provided (since, as we have seen, that can vary widely), as whether LM children receive a separate education.

There are significant organizational implications. Pupils in separate bilingual programs are typically the responsibility of a separate group of teachers and specialists who report to a separate administrative hierarchy, while LM pupils in integrated programs are the responsibility of everyone in the school. Pupils in separate bilingual programs follow a curriculum that may or may not be well-matched with what others are learning and may or may not prepare them to enter successfully into the regular program later in their school careers; while LM pupils in integrated programs are by definition studying the same content and skills as other pupils of their age and grade.

2. Many different agendas are pursued under the banner of bilingual education, and this makes it hard to sort out what is at stake in a particular discussion. Each of these agendas deserves attention, but jumbling them together, as occurs too frequently in debate, makes it impossible to address any of them adequately.

A number of educational and social objectives have been identified as justification for providing separate bilingual education programs. These include promoting "self-esteem," respecting cultural diversity, offering a safe shelter from an otherwise hostile or indifferent school environment, maintaining minority languages, providing a role for school staff drawn from language-minority groups, intervening on behalf of pupils identified as requiring special services to overcome educational disadvantages, ensuring that LM pupils are supported in participating in the full range of opportunities offered by the educational system, and ensuring academic achievement through building on the home languages of pupils. One of the goals of this article is to sort out these objectives—each will be discussed in turn—and to show that no single program can be expected to meet all of them or indeed to meet any very effectively when so overburdened with expectations.

3. To the wide spectrum of educational experiences that have been clustered under the heading of "bilingual education," and the multiple agendas (or hopes) imposed on these programs, we must add a third factor—the great diversity of pupils who are enrolled in such programs. First, there is the contrast between the youth who arrives at age 12 or 14 directly from another country and the native-born child from a language-minority family who enters kindergarten. In Western Europe, which has also experienced massive Third World immigration in recent decades, the first pupil would be placed for the first year in a transition or reception class to learn a survival proficiency in the language of the school, while the second would be assigned to a regular class, with supplemental help as needed. In Massachusetts, we tend to assign both to separate bilingual programs operating on the basis of the same educational rationale and strategy.

Second, there is the contrast, among late-arrivers, between those who have received a good education up to that point in their homeland and those from rural poverty or refugee camps, who have received little or no schooling. The difference is exponentially greater than is usually present in a classroom of children of the same age and creates tremendous problems for the teacher—and for the pupils.

Third, among younger and older pupils alike, there is the contrast between children from middle-class, highly literate homes and those from families where little reading occurs. The first group is likely to become proficiently bilingual very soon, while the second may not master either language to a level that would lead to academic success. Screening of children to determine whether they should be assigned to a separate bilingual program, as required by Massachusetts law, may result in assuming incorrectly that some "unable to perform ordinary classwork in English" (the legal test of eligibility in the state) are able to do so in Spanish or Kreyol or Lao.

Fourth (and the list could be extended), there is the contrast between children of different ethnic groups with culturally different expectations for schooling and for how children should spend their time and energies. These differences affect not only the work that children do and the rate at which they learn, but also the desire of their parents to have their children schooled through a language other than English. Typically, Asian parents are eager for their children to join the mainstream as soon as possible, while Hispanic parents are more likely to expect that the school will help to maintain their home language.

As a result of this diversity—as we will see below—the assessment of whether a particular child should be assigned to a separate program and of when pupils in separate programs are ready to be educated together with non-LM pupils has been the central administrative issue arising from our present form of bilingual education. Nearly twenty years ago James Cummins pointed out the "entry and exit fallacy in bilingual education"; this article agrees that the developmental needs of children are a continuum that should not be divided sharply into incompatible phases of separate schooling followed by "cold turkey" integration with no continuing support. Against the current practice of deciding that some LM children should be eligible for educational support through their home language and others should not, this article argues that all should be eligible to the extent that it benefits them. Against the current practice of ending such support once pupils are able to function in a regular classroom, this article argues that continued development of proficiency in a child's home language should be an option no matter how proficient he or she becomes in English.

Some years ago, as the state's equal educational opportunity official, I was asked to speak at the conference of the Massachusetts Association for Bilingual Education. If language minority pupils were integrated and held to the same high standards as other pupils, I said, I would support their continuing to be taught bilingually for as many years as their parents wished. If they were segregated and followed a separate curriculum without accountability for results, I would fight to get them out of bilingual programs as quickly as possible. That continues to be my position, and it underlies the recommendations made here.

WHAT WE CAN LEARN FROM THE NUMBERS

The education of pupils whose first language is not English is no longer a rather exotic problem for a few urban school systems but is and will increasingly be a challenge faced by most schools and most teachers.

The latest figures from the federal government, based on 1993–94 enrollments, show more than 2.1 million public school pupils reported as "Limited-English Proficient" (LEP). This represents 5.1 percent of all pupils in public schools. These LEP pupils represent 31.1 percent of all the pupils who are American Indian, Asian-American, or Hispanic.[2]

The comparable figures for Massachusetts were 33,364 pupils classified as LEP (in the language of the Massachusetts law, "unable to perform ordinary classwork in English") or 4.3 percent of the total.[3] By contrast, there are 922,239 LEP pupils or 19.2 percent of the total enrollment in California public schools. Of the American Indian, Asian-American, and Hispanic pupils in Massachusetts, 35.5 percent were classified as LEP.

"Bilingual education" is by no means the only way in which language-minority children are served by the public schools. Both nationally and in Massachusetts, more than two-thirds of Hispanic, Asian, and Native-American pupils[4] are not considered unable to perform their ordinary classwork in English. Many of these pupils lag in academic achievement for reasons having to do with home environment and other social factors and not with having a dominant language other than English. Almost all are enrolled in regular classes in their schools, as are many LEP pupils who attend schools where no special programs are offered. After all, only 11 states mandate bilingual education; another 25 make some provision for teaching English as a second language (ESL), but this is rarely done on a full-time basis, at least after the first year.

But how are LEP pupils—by definition requiring extra assistance—served if they do not attend a school with a bilingual program? The federal report shows that 85.2 percent of schools nationwide that enroll LEP pupils provide them with ESL services; only 35.5 percent provide separate bilingual programs. In other words, most of the LEP pupils are receiving help with acquisition of English without being in a full-time separate program that uses their home language. As might be expected, schools with larger proportions of minority pupils were more likely to provide separate bilingual programs.

Unfortunately, many LEP pupils still receive no services adapted to their language-acquisition needs, either in separate programs or as a supplement to participation in regular classes. A proposal a few years ago in Massachusetts to make school systems eligible for partial additional funding for language support services outside of a separate bilingual program was blocked by those who feared it would undermine the existing separate programs.

The federal report found that there were LEP pupils attending 37,419 public schools, or 46.3 percent of all public schools nationwide; 961 or nearly 60 percent of Massachusetts public schools enrolled LEP pupils. More than 1 million teachers (41.7 percent of the total) reportedly have LEP pupils in their classrooms, though for three-quarters of them the LEP pupils made up less than 10 percent of the class—two or three pupils in a typical class. Only 7.4 percent of the teachers reported that more than half of their pupils were LEP. No separate data are provided for Massachusetts, but the rates in the Northeast in general are close to the national rates.

In short, most teachers are likely at some point to have children in their classes who experience difficulty with academic work because of limited proficiency in English. Many of these pupils may also have limited academic proficiency—reading, writing, expression of complex ideas—in their first language. But few teachers have received specific training in second-language teaching. A recent federal government report found that "only 2.5 percent of teachers who instruct LEP students actually have an academic degree in ESL, or bilingual education. Furthermore, only 30 percent of the teachers with LEP students in their classes have received any training in teaching LEP students."[5]

How Are Language-Minority Pupils Doing Academically?

The picture is very mixed. As noted above, there are such different family and cultural backgrounds, such different circumstances of arrival and situation, so many personal factors of ambition or disengagement, that any generalization is likely to be wrong. Even among Hispanic pupils—the group for whom bilingual education was primarily intended—there are great differences between the average achievement of Cuban and Puerto Rican pupils, with Mexican and Central American pupils falling somewhere in between. Unfortunately, there are no good data that compare the achievement or attainment of these millions of pupils by whether they participated in separate bilingual education programs.

We do have some general information comparing the achievement of Hispanic pupils in general with those of white non-Hispanic pupils on the National Assessment of Educational Progress (NAEP). In 1992, Hispanic pupils, near the end of their schooling at age 17, were reading (in English) at about the level of white pupils at age 13; their achievement in science was comparable, that in math a little better.[6]

The school dropout rate as of 1995 for Hispanics aged 18 through 24 and born in the United States was 17.9 percent (that of immigrants was 46.2 percent), compared with 12.2 percent of blacks and 8.6 percent of whites (the dropout rates for foreign-born black and white youth were actually lower than those for the native-born). While social class and income are clearly related to school completion, black and white youth of comparable income levels drop out at about the same rate; it is disturbing to learn, however, that "Hispanic youth from families with low and middle incomes are more likely to drop out than white and black youths at the same income levels."[7]

The term "bilingual education" has come to stand for the whole question of how we should educate immigrant and other language-minority children. As a result, the fact that our schools are in general not serving Hispanic pupils very successfully tends to be blamed on bilingual programs. This is unfair to those who work in those programs. While there is much that could be criticized in the way bilingual programs have operated—especially, perhaps, that many have been forced to use staff who were inadequately trained or insufficiently proficient in the two languages—the reality is that most LM pupils have not been in bilingual programs, and that factors of home and social environment are powerfully at work in their academic difficulties.

On the other hand, there is little evidence that separate bilingual programs, where they have been implemented extensively and with adequate resources, have made a crucial difference in the academic success of LM youth. After 30 years and the schooling of millions of language-minority pupils, it is difficult to find significant differences among states that have schooled them in very different ways. Massachusetts mandates bilingual education, Delaware prohibits it, but Hispanic achievement is not notably higher in one state than in the other; indeed, the gap between Hispanic and non-Hispanic white scores on the NAEP was substantially larger in Massachusetts than it was in Delaware.

THE DEBATE: MORE HEAT THAN LIGHT

The annual debate over amending or repealing the Massachusetts law mandating bilingual education produces more heat than light; indeed, it produces very little light at all. Each year in response to proposals for change, hundreds of children from bilingual classes across the state are bused to attend the State House hearing, and legislators listen to a series of pleas not to dismantle the only program that offers these children opportunity and respect. Repeatedly over the years, the suggestion has been made that better information is needed and that the subject should be studied for a year, with action the next year. And so it goes; nothing really changes.

This extreme sensitivity about proposals for change in the bilingual education status quo was much in evidence last year, when the Massachusetts Board of Education decided to amend and simplify the regulations for bilingual education as part of a regulatory reform initiative. It should be noted that administrative regulations are not infrequently a way for advocates of a particular program to go well beyond what the legislature intended in adopting a law. Hearings on regulations do not usually attract a large turnout, but in this case, according to the Department of Education, 200 people attended in Fall River; 800 in Boston; 600 in Springfield; and 350 in Marlborough; 205—overwhelmingly defenders of bilingual education—presented testimony, and more than 200 written statements were received, together with many petitions. Why the massive response? The proposed changes did not in fact address in any way the purposes of the existing law or the nature of the instruction that should be provided to LM children. It seems likely, on the basis of the proposed changes that attracted particular comment, that the heavy turnout and opposition were aroused by proposals that would make the jobs of bilingual teachers, administrators, classroom aides, and community outreach workers less secure, even though with the increasing enrollments of language-minority pupils school systems will continue to be eager to employ all the well-qualified bilingual staff they can find.[8]

Privately, advocates of bilingual education will often concede that the law enacted in 1971 as Chapter 71A of the Massachusetts General Laws could stand some modification after more than a quarter-century, and that many local programs need to be improved, but these advocates have been unwilling to enter into open discussion about what those modifications and improvements might be. Opponents tend to dismiss the entire bilingual education effort as misguided and socially divisive. Neither side has much in the way of solid evidence on which to draw.

Nor is this accidental. Bilingual education was one of my early re-
sponsibilities when I was in charge of urban education and equal
opportunity for the Massachusetts Department of Education. When
a separate Bureau of Transitional Bilingual Education was established, I continued to work on the equity issues affecting language-
minority children and was greatly frustrated by the reluctance of my
colleagues in the bilingual education office to hold bilingual programs responsible for measurable outcomes; they did not (as the
law required) prescribe an annual test of English proficiency and
successfully resisted inclusion of bilingual program pupils in the
statewide assessments—arguing that it would be bad for their self-
esteem—or any limit on number of years in the program. In effect,
local programs could choose how they would assess the progress
of pupils. When I reviewed the records of thousands of children in
the Boston schools, I found that many of them were reported—
whether rightly or wrongly was impossible to determine—for five
or more years in the lowest category of English proficiency.

As a result, the Bilingual Education Commission appointed by Governor Weld under the provisions of the Education Reform Act found that

> despite TBE being in place in Massachusetts for 23 years, we don't know
> whether TBE is effective. In short, we do not know, on the basis of mea-
> sured outcomes, whether TBE programs in Massachusetts produce good
> results or poor results. There are no comprehensive data that evaluate the
> performance of TBE pupils compared with pupils from other groups. This
> specialized program which accounts for 5 percent of all pupils in Massa-
> chusetts public schools and 17 percent of all pupils in Boston public schools
> is not held separately accountable for its performance.[9]

Does that mean that bilingual education has failed, that it is (as
some claim) a "disaster"? No, it means that we have no idea whether
or not it has been more successful than other approaches that could
have been used. We do know that Hispanic pupils are doing rather
badly in Massachusetts schools, while pupils from some other language-minority groups who make less extended use of bilingual
education are doing rather well. It would be inappropriate to conclude, however, that, say, Chinese children on the average do better
than do Hispanic children in subsequent schooling because the
Chinese students' parents tend to avoid separate bilingual classes. It
may well be that the decisions of their parents to have them attend

regular classes reflect attitudes about education that also affect educational achievement in other ways. So we need to be cautious about interpreting the available data and skeptical about claims on both sides of the issue that "research proves" this or that about the merits of bilingual education.

We are fortunate that an extensive review of more than 30 years of research and evaluation nationwide on the schooling of language-minority pupils was published recently by the National Research Council.[10] The report found that we know much less than one would expect from an effort that has involved millions of children over the past 35 years and has been studied to death; by my calculations, about $100 million has been spent over that period on evaluation of bilingual and related programs. In particular, we can't say with confidence that it is more effective to teach children for a number of years through their home language.

The bottom line of the National Research Council report seems to be that good English-only programs are more effective than mediocre bilingual programs, and good bilingual programs are better than mediocre English-only programs. Indeed, I would go further and suggest that high-quality bilingual programs may be better than high-quality English-only programs for any child (that's why five of my own have attended a bilingual school), if only because children become proficient in two languages and in the process learn something about how to learn. But it also should lay to rest the claim that "research proves" that under all circumstances separate bilingual education is the only responsible prescription for language-minority pupils.

THE CRUCIAL QUESTIONS

Research and evaluation are not really what the controversy over bilingual education is about. A number of questions, most of them deeply felt, have been jumbled together in a way that makes it virtually impossible to talk reasonably about how to do our best for language-minority children. As a result, we have fallen back on a "one-size-fits-all" prescription. Below, in ascending order of importance, are the questions that seem most pressing:

1. Is it essential to the academic success of language-minority pupils that their self-esteem be promoted through an emphasis, in school, on their home language and culture?

Bilingual education programs are increasingly justified on the psycho-political basis that instruction primarily through the ancestral language is essential to the self-esteem and subsequent educational success of language-minority children; some advocates go so far as to urge that it be provided even to those who come to school speaking only English, since, as bilingual guru Jim Cummins wrote, "the language spoken by the child in the home is, in itself, essentially irrelevant."

Research support for this policy prescription is notably weak. For example, a study of 270 Puerto Rican children, grades 4–6, in Chicago found that"bilingual students who read only English adequately had significantly more positive self-esteem scores than those who read only Spanish adequately.... Students who had participated in a bilingual program reported significantly less positive self-esteem scores than those who had never had this type of experience.... The language of the dominant culture appears to be a key factor in the self-concept development of these students." A study of Mexican-American students in California found that those in bilingual programs had lower self-concept (and reading scores) than those in the regular program. Another found that limited-English-speaking children matched English-speaking children in self-concept and concluded,"While instruction through the native language may provide linguistic and conceptual advantages, these findings called into question one of the most frequently cited rationales for bilingual education, its positive effects on self-concept."[11]

That, surely, is the point: schools should provide high-quality bilingual programs because learning through two languages is intellectually challenging and broadens a child's horizons, not because it reinforces her self-esteem. To the extent that educators come to see the development of self-esteem in children as a primary goal in itself, they risk neglecting their primary mission of helping children achieve competence, perseverance, and optimism—the real contents of self-worth, through the achievement of the academic goals of schooling.

2. How can we (the social majority and the institutions and practices we create) show respect for minorities among us? Does this require that we actively promote alternative cultures, including the languages through which they are often expressed?

Bilingual education in Massachusetts has a strong cultural agenda, expressed for example in the provision in the law requiring that bilingual programs provide instruction

> in the history and culture of the country, territory or geographic area which is the native land of the parents of children of limited English-speaking ability who are enrolled in the program and in the history and culture of the United States. (Ch. 71A, S.1)

Anyone who has visited separate bilingual classes knows that this mandate is taken very seriously, though often with insufficient understanding of the dynamic nature of culture. Children are typically taught that "their" culture is this or that of the customs of a homeland, which may itself have changed greatly, but little about the culture their ethnic group is creating as it lives and develops in the United States. What they are taught about their "heritage" may have little to do with what their parents or grandparents knew about and valued in their homeland; for example, religion (as a system of beliefs as contrasted with folkloric practices) is rarely mentioned, even though it is central to most lived cultures. Those who have developed the curriculum rarely ask what aspects of their heritage the parents themselves are concerned to convey to their children, and what they are quite ready to abandon.

And what country's "history and culture" should be taught to children whose first language is Spanish? I visited a bilingual class made up entirely of Dominican and Puerto Rican children whose teacher had made the classroom into what can best be described as a shrine to José Martí, the poet and patriot, complete with Cuban flags, posters, and exhibits. When the Massachusetts bilingual law was enacted, we were thinking primarily of Puerto Rican (that is why "territory or geographic area" was added) and Portuguese immigrant children; today language-minority children in Massachusetts schools come from 50 or 60 different countries. Our schools should teach all children about the history and culture of countries around the world, especially those that have contributed recently to our population or have special geopolitical significance, but the schools should not provide a separate curriculum in cultural studies for separate groups.

There are good educational reasons to provide opportunities for pupils to explore particular traditions in more depth, and to seek to maintain or develop the language spoken by their parents. In a number of countries, the education system provides supplemental instruction in home language and culture on a voluntary basis as a supplement to the regular program, either in schools or in community settings.[12] In Massachusetts, the Chelsea Public Schools have chosen to do so within the after-school program; this seems entirely appropriate as a form of educational enrichment that leaves children and their parents free to decide their priorities.

3. Does a separate bilingual class provide a uniquely supportive environment?

The argument is frequently made—though usually in private—that school systems are hostile environments for language-minority pupils, except within the separate bilingual program where they are understood and valued. There is unfortunately too much truth in this stereotype to dismiss it altogether, though it is unjust to many genuinely concerned teachers and administrators. "Benign neglect" is the posture taken by many principals toward the bilingual classes in their schools; they are happy to leave responsibility for them to the school system's bilingual program director. Many teachers are equally happy not to have to worry about "those children" or to become competent in instruction for second-language development.

So there is some truth in the contention that the social and educational environment outside a separate bilingual program may be less supportive than that within it. Bilingual education teachers have told me again and again that they resist the pressure to "mainstream" the pupils entrusted to them because they are convinced that other teachers will not care about them in the same way; the children may be ready for the regular program, they say, but the regular program is not ready for them.

In the final analysis, however, this argument is unacceptable because it assumes that schools cannot and will not change to become supportive and integrated environments for all of their pupils; indeed, it implicitly gives them permission not to care. No doubt it was helpful in the 1970s to provide a separate educational setting for the newly arriving immigrant and migrant children, but increasingly we have a new generation of teachers and principals who are committed to serving minority children well. Many will need additional training in second-language acquisition, and in working collaboratively with bilingual education and ESL teachers. Principals will need help in planning for an integrated program that provides adequate language support. It will be a lot of work, but it can and must be done.

The "sheltered environment" continues to make sense when new immigrants arrive and must make an adjustment to American school life—especially if they have had little previous schooling—as well as to a new language. Those who are past elementary-school age may find this especially difficult. Reception classes and even "newcomer schools" can be very appropriate under those circumstances, provided they are not allowed to become educational dead-ends.

4. What can we do to preserve the languages spoken by immigrant groups, so that their children will be able to communicate with their parents and grandparents, and so that they will be able to use those languages vocationally and culturally as adults?

The short answer is not very much, unfortunately. Languages are typically lost in the second generation of immigration—at the latest, in the third generation—unless the immigrant group manages to isolate itself from the influence of the wider society (as exemplified by the Amish and by Hasidic Jews), despite all the good intentions of ethnic activists. The evidence is all around us, and most studies have shown that the children of immigrants from Mexico and from Southeast Asia are using English most of the time and are failing to maintain bilingualism in their children.[13]

The situation is somewhat different with "territorial language-minority groups," who are established in an area where they form such a majority that they can sustain institutions of public life that require the use of their language rather than the national language. Recently I prepared an advisory memorandum at the request of a commission working on these issues in South Africa, where there are nine major languages that have been sustained by social and geographical segregation. Massive population movements in South Africa have resulted in the mixing of language groups in ways that reduce the likelihood that some languages will maintain themselves in active public use in urban areas. Despite the strong political demand to maintain these languages through the educational system, I suggested that bilingualism is established and maintained only when each of the two languages serves a necessary social function. Languages may be taught and required in school for ideological reasons, but they are not spoken unless people have a reason to speak them. Language shift occurs inevitably when children have no reason to use the language of their parents outside the home. Policymakers should therefore make soberly informed predictions (not pious hopes) about future language use in society, asking whether each language will manage to maintain itself in a distinct sphere, and how. Language-maintenance efforts in schools should be undertaken only in conjunction with such well-founded predictions; by themselves, they will fail and waste time that should be spent on equipping pupils to function effectively in the society and economy. Families and cultural groups will, outside school, maintain elements of language and culture which they value.[14]

Here the point is simply that, if the goal of home language instruction is to maintain functional bilingualism into the second and third generation from immigration, this goal is very unlikely to be met unless there are powerful social supports outside the school—of a sort that do not commonly exist in the United States. Children who are born here to immigrant (or Puerto Rican migrant) families may speak Spanish or another language with their parents, but experience shows that they are unlikely to speak it with their children.

A strong case can be made for seeking to develop the bilingual proficiency of language-minority children as part of the regular program of instruction, especially at the intermediate and secondary level, when languages are usually taught. Language-minority pupils will not necessarily choose to develop further the language they have spoken at home, perceiving correctly that another language may be more useful to their ambitions for the future. For example, relatively few of the Turkish pupils in Berlin have taken advantage of the opportunity to study Turkish as an academic subject, preferring to learn English as a language essential to many careers. It would not be unusual if Haitian pupils in Massachusetts were to prefer to study French in high school rather than Kreyol, or if pupils whose parents came from Indochina saw little use for a high level of academic proficiency in Khmer, Lao, Hmong, or even Vietnamese, though they might be motivated to learn Chinese as a language useful to future employment.

5. Is it important that teachers of language-minority students be drawn from the same ethnic or language-minority group?

It is common in Western Europe to assign immigrant children to a "reception class" for their first year, and when possible these classes are staffed by a native speaker of their home language as well as by a native Dutch or German or Danish teacher. There are some advantages for language-minority pupils to have a teacher who does not know their language and so be forced to use the language of the school some of the time, but there are also advantages to having a teacher who can explain and advise in the pupils' home language.

This seems a wise provision, especially if the language-minority teacher also works with students schoolwide in capacities that make clear that he or she is a fully respected member of the school staff and a model of bilingual and bicultural functioning. We should welcome the growing number of school principals in Massachusetts who were bilingual education teachers or administrators. On the other hand, we should not attribute too great a significance to ethnic identity; the National Research Council study found "little empirical support for the widely held view...that teachers who are themselves members of minority groups are more effective working with children from those groups, or better able to adapt instruction to respond to cultural differences."[15]

The more significant issue is the competence of the teachers who work with language-minority pupils. It is impossible to make an accurate assessment of how proficient bilingual program staff are in English, but there is considerable anecdotal evidence that many are inadequate models of speaking and even writing for the pupils they

vely few have received specific
econd language. The Bilingual
)f 2,346 bilingual program staff
y, 65 percent were certified in
grams for some language groups
the majority of the teachers were
certification. Many bilingual pro-
der regulations adopted in 1982,
age and culture test but not to
tional methods and materials;
ito effect in October 1994, but
teachers.[16]

Massachusetts faces the same problem with many teachers of English as a second language. Until 1982, there was no state certification in that specialization, and until 1993 any teacher who had been certified in elementary education or in English could be "grandfathered" as an ESL teacher without specific training. Not until 1994 was a system put in place to recertify these hundreds of teachers on the basis of specific training in ESL methods. Special education and Chapter 1 (compensatory education) teachers who work with language-minority pupils are rarely trained in second-language acquisition.[17] In short, there is a major shortfall of trained competence among non-bilingual staff who work with language-minority pupils, as there is among bilingual program staff. Few principals of schools enrolling LEP pupils have received training in the requirements of a sound program of second-language development.

6. Must intervening on behalf of language-minority pupils require segregating them?

The political and administrative battles in recent years have been fought primarily over the criteria and process for entry and exit to and from bilingual programs, and not (as they should be) over what quality and scope of instruction is provided. It would be far more productive to discuss the services that should be made available to language-minority pupils as they participate in the regular school program. Some of these services might be provided on a pull-out basis in separate groups, others might involve modifications of the staffing, instruction, and work in the regular classroom.

It should not be assumed that an integrated approach to the education of language-minority pupils will make bilingual staff unnecessary; to the contrary, they will be essential members of the team in any school that enrolls LEP pupils—as we have seen, nearly 60 percent of all schools in Massachusetts. After all, there is no reason that a teacher who is competent to teach, say, the fourth-grade curriculum in a bilingual program and is proficient in English should not be assigned a regular fourth-grade class that includes LEP pupils. Any teacher who would not be competent to teach a regular class should not be entrusted with a bilingual program class!

The emphasis should shift from an in/out decision about enrollment in a separate bilingual program to an ongoing assessment of how best to teach the individual language-minority child as his or her language and academic and social skills develop or stagnate. The classroom teacher should have the tools to make this assessment, but should be backed up by curriculum specialists and administrators who are well briefed on what is required.

7. How can we best ensure that LM pupils are supported in participating in the full range of opportunities offered by the educational system?

The structural impediments to equal opportunity in education for language-minority pupils can best be removed by enrolling them in regular classes and treating them like other pupils, with supplemental support as needed and with supplemental opportunities, on a voluntary basis, to develop further their skills in their home language.

This is not to pretend that barriers would entirely fall away, but they would be the informal barriers that only persistent and skillful attention can remove. Discrimination on the basis of ethnic identity and of perceived competence related to proficiency in English will continue to be a problem, as will cultural miscommunication and lack of confidence on the part of some language-minority pupils. At least, however, the sense of inhabiting parallel but separate universes would be removed, as would the scheduling conflicts that often keep pupils in bilingual and regular programs apart.

Children who arrive in this country after the primary grades, especially those who have not attended school in their homeland and whose parents have little formal education, may well need a transition program of a year or more before they can be expected to benefit much from a regular classroom, however enriched with support. Reception classes of the sort that Massachusetts cities offered to an earlier wave of immigrants[18] and that most Western nations provide, and "newcomer" high schools of the sort New York, San Francisco, and other ports of entry provide, can be useful short-term measures.

8. Is it essential that children be taught reading and other skills first through their home language as a basis for developing the same skills in English?

Here we come to the central claim made for separate bilingual programs, that children who reach a high level of academic competence in their first language are more likely to be successful subsequently in a second language. Advocates argue that tremendous damage is done to children if they are not taught to read first in their home language before beginning systematic instruction in English. Early exposure to English in school for language-minority students is opposed by many bilingual education advocates, often arguing in justification that children with a solid academic background in their first language acquired before coming to the United States tend to do better at academic work in English than do children without such a background. That seems like common sense. Skills do transfer. If every language-minority pupil in Massachusetts schools had received a first-rate education for a number of years in another language, and was immersed in an environment in which that language was reinforced at every turn, the task of schools would be straightforward, and the original intention of Chapter 71A—to allow language-minority pupils to continue to study algebra or history in, say, Portuguese while learning English—would not be excessively difficult to fulfill.

The problem is that most language-minority pupils do not fit that pattern. Many were born here or came before school age and have been exposed to English in many ways; it is naïve to imagine that a bilingual program for five to seven years (the period commonly urged by advocates) can make them equivalent in home-language proficiency to children who had as many years of schooling in another country. Others are older but received little formal schooling before immigrating; they have few academic skills to transfer from their first language. To devote a number of years of American schooling to providing a teenager with solid academic skills in a language he speaks in an idiomatic form in order then to help him to transfer those skills to English may bring him to the end of his schooling before he has learned anything that will help him to get a job.

In short, the theory of the transfer of skills developed in the first language is a good one, but it does not necessarily follow that the child's American school should pretend for five to seven years that the child is still in Honduras or Somalia. Nor would this be likely to work. "It is clear," the National Research Council study notes,

> that many children first learn to read in a second language without serious negative consequences. These include children in early-immersion, two-way, and English as a second language (ESL)-based programs in North America, as well as those in formerly colonial countries that have maintained the official language [of the colonizer] as the medium of instruction, immigrant children in Israel, children whose parents opt for elite international schools, and many others.... The high literacy achievement of Spanish-speaking children in English-medium Success for All schools...that feature carefully-designed direct literacy instruction suggests that even children from low-literacy homes can learn to read in a second language if the risk associated with poor instruction is eliminated.[19]

Later, indeed, the authors conclude candidly that "we do not yet know whether there will be long-term advantages or disadvantages to initial literacy instruction in the primary language versus English, given a very high-quality program of known effectiveness in both cases."[20]

That does not mean, of course, that there may not be solid advantages to the use of the home language in at least the early stages of a child's schooling. What is above all important is that children make active use of any language with increasing skill and complexity. They are more likely to do so when stimulated to use a language with which they are already familiar. However, there is no reason to shelter children from the language on which later academic success will depend, and it should be used to an increasing extent as the medium of instruction. We should beware of claims that "research proves" that children should be instructed primarily through their home language for up to half of their years of schooling before joining their fellow pupils in a common curriculum. Well-taught, children adapt to a second language with remarkable speed and without harm to their intellectual development.

CONCLUSION

Integrating second-language learners while giving them the opportunity to continue to develop proficiency in their first language on a supplemental basis is true bilingual education. It provides them the opportunity to speak and read and write in the home language without being isolated from other pupils and what they are learning, or "sheltered" from the use of English, or held to lower expectations. The only rationale for bilingual education that is likely to be effective in the long run is that learning several languages is preferable to learning only one. "It cannot survive long as an adjunct program which bears close resemblance to makeshift measures intended to meet only transient needs," Diego Castellanos has warned. "Neither can it survive as a 'special' program for a minority group. It desperately needs the support of the wider community as part and parcel of the total educational system."[21]

Language-minority pupils—like majority pupils—should receive instruction through the minority language only if that instruction is serious and disciplined, not dilettantish or concerned more with promoting good feelings than with training minds. And it should never be a substitute for mastering curriculum content and meeting educational standards. As the author wrote in a 1988 Massachusetts government report,

> Instruction in the home language of linguistic minority students has been promoted largely as a means of assisting the transition to English. There is a better reason: that it has the potential of providing a higher-quality all-around education. Students are more likely to grapple with challenging material, to take intellectual risks, to apply themselves fully to learning if they feel secure in the language they are using. We can teach industrial arts in simplified English, but not philosophy, and the civics discussion that has to limit itself to a 700-word vocabulary will not train much of a citizen.

But instruction in the home language is justified only if it is purposeful, demanding, and accountable for results; it must not be a backwater. It is most likely to have these characteristics if it looks toward secondary-school courses, including the option of advanced placement in the home language. Study in the home language must be considered intellectually demanding and not simply remedial...

To define the education of linguistic minority students primarily in terms of their acquisition of English is too narrow. The [State] Board has adopted nine goals for education in Massachusetts, and each of these may be sought in the language with which children come to school as well as in English. It should never be the intention of teachers to suppress or devalue the language used in the home.

Our expectation should be that every linguistic minority student will acquire a solid proficiency in English and a well-rounded education. Maintenance of the first language and of the heritage culture are matters for individual choice, but public schools should ensure that there is a real opportunity to make that choice.[22]

To realize these high ambitions, the "separate development" strategy that has produced such disappointing results in bilingual education must be abandoned. Developing and maintaining proficiency in languages other than English should be seen as a valuable dimension of the overall mission of fine schools.

The damaging but too-common assumption that instruction through the home language is the solution to all the educational needs of language-minority children should be replaced by the understanding that language-minority children have a full spectrum of needs and strengths that extends far beyond language acquisition. Justice demands the commitment of the whole school team to meeting those needs and to building upon those strengths.

RECOMMENDATIONS

1. Schools should abandon efforts to promote pupil self-esteem that are extrinsic to their academic mission, while missing no opportunity to recognize the real achievements of their pupils, including those unable to reach the highest performance levels. School ethos should constantly communicate to pu-

pils, parents, and the community that nothing less than consistent effort to the best of each pupil's ability is acceptable.
2. The overall curriculum should reflect the cultural diversity of
the United States and encourage respect for differences of
religious belief and family custom. The primary emphasis,
however, should be on what we share rather than what di-
vides us, and on how it can serve as a basis for negotiating
our differences. Schools should avoid conveying the message that language-minority children and their families stand
outside the mainstream of American life.
3. Schools should consider providing special assemblies, classroom visits, and (in the upper grades) extra-curricular activities to explore particular traditions that are of interest to
groups of pupils, whether or not they share the same ethnic
background. At the secondary level, elective courses can provide a more in-depth study of the history and culture of countries or groups of countries from which pupils or their forebears
immigrated.
4. It should be made clear at every level that LEP pupils are the
responsibility of everyone in the school and the school system.
5. Consistent with the Massachusetts and national educational
goals, the quality and seriousness of language instruction in
schools should be greatly improved, and language-minority
pupils in particular should be encouraged to make a commitment to developing a high level of formal proficiency in
two or more languages.
6. Career and occupational education programs, especially those
enrolling language-minority pupils, should place a strong
emphasis on the vocational advantages of real bilingual competence.
7. All newly certified teachers, administrators, and other educational personnel should be required to show that they have
learned about how most effectively to educate LEP and other
language-minority pupils, either through coursework or
through experience with provision for demonstrating competence.
8. School systems should provide transitional reception classes
of a year—two in exceptional circumstances—for late-arriv-
ing immigrant children. The emphasis of such classes should
be on preparing pupils to participate effectively in the regu-

lar school program; they should not seek to become a substitute for that program.

NOTES

1. To keep this text uncluttered with hundreds of references, the author refers the reader who seeks documentation or more information on this and subsequent statements to Charles L. Glenn and Ester J. de Jong, *Educating immigrant children: Schools and language minorities in 12 nations* (New York: Garland, 1996). Recent statistical sources, however, will be referenced.

2. National Center for Education Statistics, "1993-94 Schools and staffing survey: A profile of policies and practices for limited english proficient students: Screening methods, program support, and teacher training" (NCES 97-472), Washington: U.S. Department of Education, February 1997, p. 6.

3. These designations are essentially synonymous.

4. Unfortunately, the categories by which school enrollment data are reported do not allow us to identify some of the other groups of which some proportion of the pupils are unable to perform classwork in English. For example, Haitian and Cape Verdean pupils are reported under "black" and Russian pupils under "white."

5. "1993-94 Schools and staffing survey," p. 16.

6. National Center for Education Statistics, *The educational progress of hispanic students (NCES 95-767)*, U.S. Department of Education, Washington, D.C., September 1995, p. 6.

7. National Center for Education Statistics, *Dropout rates in the United States: 1995 (NCES 97-473)*, U.S. Department of Education, Washington, D.C., February 1997, pp. 17, 29.

8. Despite the modesty of the proposed changes, my children brought home fliers from their bilingual school in Boston warning that the State Board was proposing to abolish bilingual education.

9. Bilingual Education Commission, *Striving for success: The education of bilingual pupils*, Commonwealth of Massachusetts, Boston, December 1994, p. 41.

10. Diane August and Kenji Hakuta (eds.), *Improving schooling for language-minority children: A research agenda*, National Research Council, Washington, D.C., 1997.

11. For references, see Glenn and de Jong, p. 306.

12. See Glenn and de Jong, chapter 7, for details.

13. See Glenn and de Jong, chapter 5, for an extended discussion and references.

14. Memo to Professor Jan De Groof, September 12, 1997.

15. August and Hakuta, p. 269.

16. Bilingual Education Commission, p. 32.

17. Ibid., p. 33.

18. See, for example, Commission on Immigration, *The problem of immigration in Massachusetts,* Massachusetts House of Representatives, Boston, 1914.

19. August and Hakuta, p. 60.

20. Ibid., p. 179.

21. Diego Castellanos with Pamela Leggio, *The best of two worlds: Bilingual/ bicultural education in the U.S.,* New Jersey State Department of Education, Trenton, 1983, p. 266.

22. Charles L. Glenn, *Educating linguistic minority students,* Office of Educational Equity, Quincy, Massachusetts, 1988, pp. 14-15.

Appendix A

Excerpts from Chapter 71A	Proposed Revisions
From Section 1. Definitions. "Children of limited English-speaking ability," (1) children who were not born in the United States whose native tongue is a language other than English and who are incapable of performing ordinary classwork in English; and (2) children who were born in the United States of non-English speaking parents and who are incapable of performing ordinary classwork in English.	"Children of limited English-speaking ability," (a) children who were not born in the United States whose native tongue is a language other than English and who are incapable of performing ordinary classwork in English; and (b) children who were born in the United States of non-English-speaking parents and who are incapable of performing ordinary classwork in English but capable of performing ordinary classwork in another language.
"Teacher of transitional bilingual education," a teacher with a speaking and reading ability in a language other than English in which bilingual education is offered and with communicative skills in English.	"Teacher of bilingual education," a teacher with a speaking and reading ability in a language other than English, in which bilingual education is offered in Massachusetts, and sufficient proficiency in English to teach through English.
"Program in transitional bilingual education," a full-time program of instruction (1) in all those courses or subjects which a child is required by law to receive and which are required by the child's school committee which shall be given in the native language of the children of limited English-speaking ability who are enrolled in the program and also in English, (2) in the reading and writing of the native language of the children of limited English-speaking ability who are enrolled in the program and in the oral comprehension, speaking, reading and writing of English, and (3) in the history and culture of the country, territory or geographic area which is the native land of the parents of children of limited English-speaking ability who are enrolled in the program and in the history and culture of the United States.	"Bilingual education," instructional and other services (a) in all those courses or subjects which a child is required by law to receive and which are required by the child's school committee which shall be given in English and with the support of the native language of the children of limited English-speaking ability; and (b) in the reading and writing of the native language of the children of limited English-speaking ability who are enrolled in the program and in the oral comprehension, speaking, reading and writing of English. [Section 1 should be amended to remove section (c). There should not be separate curriculum standards and objectives for language-minority pupils, apart from attention to language proficiency.]

Appendix A (cont'd)

Excerpts from Chapter 71A	Proposed Revisions
From Section 2. Language classification of children; establishment of program	
When, at the beginning of any school year, there are within a city, town or school district not including children who are enrolled in existing private school systems, twenty or more children of limited English-speaking ability in any such language classification, the school committee shall establish, for each classification, a program in transitional bilingual education for the children therein; provided, however, that a school committee may establish a program in transitional bilingual education with respect to any classification with less than twenty children therein.	When, at the beginning of any school year, there are within a city, town or school district, not including children who are enrolled in existing private school systems, twenty or more children of limited English-speaking ability in any such language classification, the school committee shall provide bilingual instructional and other services for these children.
Every school-age child of limited English-speaking ability not enrolled in existing private school systems shall be enrolled and participate in the program in transitional bilingual education established for the classification to which he belongs by the city, town or school district in which he resides for a period of three years or until such time as he achieves a level of English language skills which will enable him to perform successfully in classes in which instruction is given only in English, whichever shall first occur.	Bilingual instructional and other services may be provided to any pupils for whom these are educationally beneficial, subject to the approval of their parents. [Section 2, paragraphs 4, 5 and 6 should be eliminated as unnecessary once bilingual education has become part of the regular instructional program of schools for which it is appropriate as a result of the presence of LEP pupils.]
Section 3. Notice of enrollment; content; rights of parents	[Section 3 should be eliminated as unnecessary, since pupils will not be entering and leaving a separate program. The procedural safeguards appropriate to children with special needs would of course continue to apply.]

Appendix A (cont'd)

Excerpts from Chapter 71A	Proposed Revisions
Section 4. Non-resident children; enrollment and tuition; joint programs	[Section 4 should be eliminated, since inter-district transfers and out-of-district enrollment are covered by other provisions of state law.]

From Section 5. Participation in extracurricular activities of public schools; placement

Instruction in courses of subjects included in a program of transitional bilingual education which are not mandatory may be given in a language other than English. In those courses or subjects in which verbalization is not essential to an understanding of the subject matter, including but not necessarily limited to art, music and physical education, children of limited English-speaking ability shall participate fully with their English-speaking contemporaries in the regular public school classes provided for said subjects. Each school committee of every city, town or school district shall ensure to children enrolled in a program in transitional bilingual education practical and meaningful opportunity to participate fully in the extra-curricular activities of the regular public schools in the city, town or district. Programs in transitional bilingual education shall, whenever feasible, be located in the regular public schools of the city, town or the district rather than separate facilities.	Instruction in courses or subjects may be given in a language other than English. In those courses or subjects in which verbalization is not essential to an understanding of the subject matter, including but not necessarily limited to art, music and physical education, children of limited English-speaking ability shall participate fully with their English-speaking contemporaries in the regular public school classes provided for said subjects. Each school committee of every city, town or school district shall ensure to pupils of limited proficiency in English practical and meaningful opportunity to participate fully in the extra-curricular activities of the regular public schools in the city, town or district.
Children enrolled in a program of transitional bilingual education whenever possible shall be placed in classes with children of approximately the same age and level of educational attainment. If children of different age groups or educational levels are	Pupils of limited proficiency in English whenever possible shall be placed in classes with children of approximately the same age and level of educational attainment. If children of different age groups or educational levels are combined, the school committee so combining shall ensure that the instruction given each child is appropriate to his or her level of educational attainment and the city, town or the school districts shall keep adequate records of the educational level and progress of each child enrolled in a program.

Appendix A (cont'd)

Excerpts from Chapter 71A	Proposed Revisions
combined, the school committee so combining shall ensure that the instruction given each child is appropriate to his or her level of educational attainment and the city, town or the school districts shall keep adequate records of the educational level and progress of each child enrolled in a program.	The board of education, hereinafter called the board, shall grant certificates to teachers of bilingual education who possess such qualifications as are prescribed in this section. Teachers of bilingual education, including those serving under exemptions as provided in this section, shall be compensated by local school committees not less than a step on the regular salary schedule applicable to permanent teachers certified under section thirty-eight G of chapter 71.

The maximum student-teacher ratio shall be set by the department and shall reflect the special educational needs of children enrolled in programs in trasitional bilingual education.

The board shall grant certificates to teachers of bilingual education who present the board with satisfactory evidence that they (a) possess a speaking and reading ability in a language other than English, in which bilingual education is offered in Massachusetts, and sufficient proficiency in English to teach through English, as determined by the board; (b) are in good health, provided that no applicant shall be disqualified because of blindness or defective hearing; (c) are of sound moral character; (d) possess a bachelor's degree or an earned higher academic degree; (e) meet such requirements as to courses of study, semester hours therein, experience, training, and demonstrated competence as may be required by the board; and (f) are legally present in the United States and possess legal authorization for employment. They shall not be subject to the requirement of section 38G that they be American citizens.

From Section 6. Teacher's certification and certificate; qualifications and requirements; compensation; exemptions

The board shall grant certificates to teachers of transitional bilingual education who present the board with satisfactory evidence that they (1) possess a speaking and reading ability in a language, other than English, in which bilingual education is offered and communicative skills in English; (2) are in good health, provided that no applicant shall be disqualified because of blindness or defective hearing; (3) are of sound moral character; (4) possess a bachelor's degree or an earned higher academic degree or are graduates of a normal school approved by the board; (5) meet such requirements as to courses of study, semester hours therein, experience and training as may be required by the board; and (6) are legally present in the United States and possess legal authorization for employment.

[The remaining paragraphs of this section and the remaining sections of Chapter 71A should remain or be removed as judged appropriate; they do not affect the quality of education provided.]

Welcoming Remarks by James Peyser, Pioneer Institute, and John Silber, Boston University, at the READ Institute/Pioneer Institute Conference October 30, 1998, at Boston University

New Directions in Educating Language-Minority Children:
An Agenda for the Future

James Peyser: I want to welcome you all here this morning for what I think will be a very interesting and very important conference.

We have a very impressive group of people here today representing policymakers, educators, scholars from around the Commonwealth and, indeed, across the country. And I'm not talking just about the speakers and the panelists, but also those of you who are attending and are participating by your attendance at the conference this morning. Indeed, one of the real values of this group is not just, again, the expertise that will be present up on the stage, but the expertise that's out in the audience, and we hope to be able to tap into that and have some very useful discussion as the day goes on.

My job here today is essentially to get everyone seated and to introduce our host, who is the Chancellor of Boston University and its former President, John Silber. He is also the Chairman of the Massachusetts Board of Education.

John Silber is not someone who needs much of an introduction, whether it's here in Massachusetts or anywhere else, but there are a few things that you may not know about him, with regard especially to this conference, but also with regard to his work in the area of kindergarten through twelfth-grade education and education reform.

He has a lifelong involvement and commitment in education; you might say this is embedded in his genes since his mother was a school teacher from age 18 to age 82. It was perhaps inescapable that John get involved in education.

You may not know that he was instrumental in the launch of Operation Head Start, and that he was involved in the drafting of the original bilingual education statutes at the federal level by Senator Ralph Yarborough of Texas.

John Silber has been a leader in Massachusetts in the area of bilingual education and has helped put it back on the agenda here.

We at Pioneer and the READ Institute are very grateful to Boston University for hosting this event, and we are honored to have John Silber here with us this morning.

John Silber: As Chancellor of Boston University, I'm delighted to welcome you to this important conference. Boston University is honored to provide a site for this work, and a site for further outreach by the Pioneer Institute, which has a remarkable history of looking at the facts, attempting to understand the facts, and then using the facts to design policy proposals. It is an organization of extraordinary rationality in a society that is not always rational in the way in which it goes about its business. The Pioneer Institute gathers the evidence, assimilates the arguments, and tries to come up with policies that make sense and that are compelling by virtue of their intellectual clarity, coherence, and their humility before the facts of the situation. I also want to compliment the institute for having helped the READ Institute get its start.

The subject of our conference is of course one that's very important. Bilingual education could be a threat to equality of opportunity, or it could be a vehicle for equality of opportunity. It is especially important with regard to bilingual education that we try to agree on the points that we have in common so that we can focus on our differences without leading to confusion.

I suppose we all agree that English is the *de facto* language of the United States. If this country were to go in the direction of official bilingualism, with more than one language as the official language of our country, we would face all the troubles that are faced by Canada, Belgium, and India. If, therefore, we are going to support English as the at least *de facto* language of this country, how are we going to do it?

We ought to agree that every child in the United States has the right to learn English as quickly as possible. This is part and parcel of a child's birthright as an American. I don't know how we can give meaning to equality of opportunity if children do not have the opportunity to learn English quickly, at as early an age as possible. I don't know any way that a person can have equality of opportunity if he or she is unable to speak the common national language.

My father came to this country in 1902 as a young sculptor working on the German Pavilion in the St. Louis World's Fair of 1904. He knew no English; his language was German. It was quite adequate for the construction of the German Pavilion because all the other workers were German. But after the facility had been completed and the Fair was opened, my father sought other employment. He thought of this country as a land of 1,000 possibilities, and he was going to try to make his way here as an American citizen.

Walking down the street, he saw a sign that said "undertaker." Undertaker, if you translate it directly into German is "*unternehmer*," and an *unternehmer* in German is a contractor or an entrepreneur. Since he was an architect and a builder, he thought, "Well, this is a way I can make contact with architects and builders." So he went into the undertaker's establishment, only to find himself surrounded by coffins. "At this point," he told me, "I decided I had to learn English as quickly as possible." And that's what he did.

I think this is a second point on which we can agree: Every American child has the right to equality of opportunity, and equality of opportunity requires facility in the English language.

Third, although the best way to make all children literate in English is a matter of controversy, the purpose of bilingual education is to use the first language of the child to facilitate learning English. Whatever our opinion about the best method, we recognize that the goal of bilingual education is to accelerate the acquisition of the English language.

I would suppose that all of us can agree on these three points. I can say this: When Senator Yarborough introduced legislation on bilingual education, his purpose was to assist Spanish-speaking children of Texas, helping them learn English as quickly as possible. He became involved in bilingual education as a result of work done by my students in a slum project that I required of all students in my courses at the University of Texas. I would send those students into four blocks of the worst slums in their hometown and ask them to visit every home, talk to every person who lived there. Then the students were to find out who owned the slum property and visit all the owners. The students were to ask those who lived in slums, "Why do you live in slums?" They were to ask the owners, "Why do you own slum property?" They were to ask city officials, "What are you doing to uphold the laws, sanitation codes, et cetera, with regard to this property?" And they were also required to visit the schools nearest the slums and see what they were like.

In visiting the schools, one student talked to a teacher who was on the threshold of retirement. She said she would retire the next year. That imaginative student said, "If you had one wish that could be fulfilled before you retire as a teacher, what would it be?" She said, "My wish would be very simple. I would like to come to class and say, 'Children, pick up your pencils.' As it is, I have to say, 'Children, this is a pencil, now pick up your pencils.'" Those children had never seen a pencil, and the only word they knew for pencil, if they knew it at all, was "lapiz."

I told that story to Senator Yarborough. He said, "Dr., is it that bad?" And I said, "Senator, it's that bad." And that was the beginning of his commitment to bilingual education. It was for one purpose only— to teach English as quickly as possible.

His view was seconded by Ernesto Ortiz, a ranch foreman in Texas, who said, "My children go to school to learn Spanish so they can grow up to be busboys and waiters. I teach them English at home so they can grow up to be doctors or lawyers."

I don't wish to anticipate the conclusions of this important conference by getting into my own views on the subject. Many of you have a suspicion about what they might be in any case. But I do wish you well in these deliberations. Again, my thanks to the Pioneer Institute and to the READ Institute, and I wish you a very successful conference.

Panel I—What the Research Tells Us

Moderator, Professor Charles L. Glenn, Boston University

Charles L. Glenn: My name is Charles Glenn, and I teach educational policy here at Boston University. Since Chancellor Silber was reminiscing, I might mention that I was the first director of bilingual education here in Massachusetts back in the early 1970s, and that I have sent five of my own children to the Rafael Hernandez Bilingual School in Boston.

The focus of this panel reflects a peculiarity of American educational policy, and that is its very heavy reliance upon research and upon claims about research to justify policies. There are millions of children in the world who are educated bilingually. There are educational systems that educate bilingually as a matter of policy—in Catalonia in Spain, in Wales, in Friesland in the Netherlands, and in many other places.

The difference in American educational policy is that in a number of the most significant states, as far as language-minority populations are concerned, the decision to educate children bilingually is not based on any real discussion about whether bilingualism is desirable or not desirable, whether it ought to be promoted by government or allowed to happen as a result of the choices of individuals, families, and communities about what language they'll use.

The difference in the American situation is that policy is based, and has been based for more than twenty years, upon claims that only through teaching language-minority children through their home language is it possible to promote their learning English effectively and their becoming cognitively developed.

Research claims have been at the heart of the American practice of bilingual education, and it's necessary that we start this conference with an exploration of those claims. Diane August is an important participant because she was the co-director of what I believe is the most extensive effort ever to look at all of the research and all of the

40

experience of bilingual education in the United States, and to reach some conclusions about areas in which we know or we do not know what works and what does not work. The project which she co-directed with Kenji Hakuta of Stanford University, on behalf of the National Research Council, is one of the most significant landmarks in the evolution of this debate.

IMPROVING CAPACITY AND EDUCATIONAL ACCOUNTABILITY IN SCHOOLS SERVING ENGLISH LANGUAGE LEARNERS

Diane August: Thank you for giving me the opportunity to be here, and to share my thoughts with you. I have been asked to talk about some of the findings from the National Academy of Sciences report, *Improving Schooling for Language Minority Children,*[1] that are relevant to the agenda of this meeting which is New Directions in Educating Language-Minority Children: An Agenda for the Future. In the brief time that I have to share some of the findings of the report with you, I want to highlight three areas that I think are crucial to improving the education of these children: the first is ensuring all teachers are prepared to educate English language learners; the second entails aligning curriculum and instruction with high academic standards and providing schools with the resources they need to help these children meet the standards; and the third consists of assessing English language learners to determine whether they are making progress toward meeting high academic standards.

As my colleague Charles Glenn notes in his paper "Rethinking Bilingual Education," more than 1 million teachers (41.7 percent of the total) reportedly have English language learners in their classrooms. Thus, most teachers are likely at some point to have children in their classes who experience difficulty with academic work because of limited proficiency in English. But few teachers have received specific training in second language teaching. A recent federal government report found that only 2.5 percent of teachers who instruct English language learners actually have an academic degree in ESL, or bilingual education. Furthermore, only 30 percent of the teachers with English language learners in their classes have received any training in teaching these students.[2] There is a need to prepare all those entering, and already working in, the teaching profession—regardless of background—to meet the linguistic and subject matter needs of English language learners. It will be a challenging task, however, to prepare all teachers who work with culturally and linguistically diverse populations to have the specialized knowledge and skills required to deal effectively with the special circumstances, experiences, and backgrounds of these children. For example, besides being well-versed in the subject matter they are teaching, experts recommend that teachers be knowledgeable about first and second language acquisition, strategies compatible and supportive of the cultural backgrounds of second language learners, and second language teaching methodology. In addition, teachers who teach English language learners should be fluent in the language of instruction and able to use that language effectively in the subject areas that they teach.

The NAS report identified four programs that represent a variety of staff development efforts including continuing education (Cooperative Learning in Bilingual Settings, ESOL in-service project), recruitment (Latino Teacher Project), pre-service education (Latino Teacher Project), and credentialing (CLAD program).

The Cooperative Learning in Bilingual Settings program trains teachers to use an empirically validated method of teaching. Teachers receive intensive professional development in the Cooperative Integrated Reading and Composition (CIRC) instructional model, an approach developed at Johns Hopkins University to promote students' acquisition of literacy. The staff development effort stresses a comprehensive approach in which teachers are provided with content knowledge (how to implement the CIRC model), as well as practice through supervision. A key emphasis of the project is on inquiry-based learning, in which teachers engage in peer coaching and collaboration with colleagues. The project highlights the importance of follow-up support systems.

A second model, the Latino Teacher Project, is an effort to target minority populations to increase the pool of bilingual teachers in Central Los Angeles by creating a career ladder for Latino teaching assistants. Staff development efforts are based on a "community of learners" model in which participants are assisted and assist each other in progressing through teacher education programs.

A third model, the ESOL in-service project, designed to assist all teachers serving English language learners in Florida, provides teachers with courses to help them better educate these students. Coursework includes methods of teaching ESL, cross-cultural communication and understanding, and testing and evaluation of English language learners. Program staff are engaged in ongoing efforts to tailor the courses to meet the diverse needs of a heterogeneous group of teachers.

And the fourth model, the CLAD Program, is an effort to reform state staff development and credentialing programs in California. It is geared to giving all teachers who work with English language learners the skills and knowledge necessary to be effective. To add the CLAD endorsement to their license, already-credentialed teachers must pass examinations in (1) language structure and first and second language development, (2) special methods of instruction for English language learners, and (3) cultural diversity. Teachers need the CLAD endorsement to instruct English language learners.

The second area I will briefly touch on is curriculum and instruction. All too often, English language learners are marginalized and provided with curriculum or instruction that is not aligned with district or state content standards. It is crucial that English language learners be held to the same high standards as other children. However, setting high expectations for English language learners will further the cause of educational equity, but only if appropriate, high-quality instruction and other essential resources are available. The NRC report dedicates a chapter to effective schoolwide and classroom practices. Examples include a customized learning environment in which staff design programs to reflect school and community contextual factors and goals while meeting the diverse needs of students, instructional strategies to ensure that English language learners comprehend instruction, and staff development for all teachers in the school who have contact with English language learners.

The third area I will briefly discuss is assessment. Assessment issues will be framed in the context of standards-based reform because I believe that this is the most promising approach to improving schooling for all children, including English language learners. States, districts, and schools need accurate information about the academic progress of English language learners to determine whether they are making progress toward meeting district and state performance standards. Assessment systems that fully incorporate English language learners should include the following:

1. Identification of English language learners who can take the standard English assessments and methods to ensure that such students are assessed using these instruments.

2. Determination of assessment alternatives for English language learners for whom the standard English assessment is not appropriate. Possible methods include the use of native language assessments for those students for whom these assessments are appropriate, or alternative forms of performance assessments in English.

3. Setting a limit on how long English language learners can be excluded from taking the same performance assessments in English as their English speaking peers. Experts have suggested that this limit be based on their levels of English proficiency rather than years in school or in English-only programs.

4. Collection of data on students' performance in the content areas for students in the school as a whole, disaggregated by English language learner status of the students.

5. Use of this data to make decisions regarding school improvement.

Implementing these recommendations poses many challenges. Two examples follow. First, many states currently base their decision on whether to include English language learners in standard English assessments on the number of years they have attended an English-speaking school. This method is problematic, however, because it does not take into account the fact that individual students vary greatly in their rate of English acquisition. Thus, even if the number of years were set at the accurate average time it takes for learning the English adequate for the assessment, it would inappropriately exclude a large number of fast learners of English and inappropriately include a large number of students who need more time to acquire English. A better-calibrated approach would be the use of an assessment of English proficiency that measures all four domains of proficiency (listening, speaking, reading, and writing) as part of a triage system that would determine whether to offer unmodified English assessment, modi-fied English assessment, or a temporary waiver from assessment. However, the use of current English proficiency measures for this pur-pose is not without problems—these assessments take additional time to administer, and many English language proficiency assessments have not been"benchmarked"for this purpose. Methods also need to be developed to determine assessment alternatives for those English language learners who do not take the standard English assessment.

A second issue revolves around how to determine whether English language learners are making adequate progress toward meeting dis-trict or state performance standards. Making this determination re-quires a definition of adequate yearly progress for English language learners and the disaggregation of data by English proficiency status. In terms of definition of progress, the same high performance standards that are established for all students are the ultimate goal for English lan-guage learners. English language learners, however, may take more time to meet these standards (especially those children with limited prior schooling). As such, additional benchmarks toward these standards will probably need to be developed to assess the progress of English lan-guage learners in meeting these standards. Disaggregating data by En-glish language learner status with the purpose of generalizing beyond a particular sample poses methodological challenges. When the num-bers of such students are small and there is a need to generalize beyond the particular sample, such as through a comparison of a sample of third-graders this year with a sample of third-graders from the previous year, statistical soundness will be threatened by small sample sizes.

Given the increasing numbers of English language learners and their poor school performance, it is critical that resources—both intellectual and financial—be allocated to address the issues raised in this paper. It is time to put aside our differences and work on the areas where there is consensus. As Jay Greene points out in his meta-analysis of studies of bilingual education, the use of the native language is an effective instruc-tional technique,[3] but it only takes care of one-fifth of the task of effec-tively educating language-minority students. Many other things need to happen to effectively educate these children, including those that have been raised in this article. It is time we turn to them now.

Thank you.

NOTES

1. August, D. and Hakuta, K. (editors) (1997). *Improving schooling for language minority children: A research agenda.* Washington, D.C.: The National Academy of Sciences Press.

2. National Center for Education Statistics. (1997). *"1993-1994 Schools and staffing survey: A profile of policies and practices for limited English proficient students."* Washington, D.C: U.S. Department of Education, p.16.

3. Greene, Jay, P. (1998). *A meta-analysis of the effectiveness of bilingual education.* Austin, Texas: The Public Policy Clinic of the Department of Government at the University of Texas.

MYSTERY ON THE BILINGUAL EXPRESS:
A CRITIQUE OF THE THOMAS AND COLLIER STUDY

Charles Glenn: The next panelist is Professor Christine H. Rossell, a political scientist at Boston University, who has not only written and published extensively about bilingual education research and other issues of education policy, but has also served frequently in court cases as an expert witness on this subject.

Christine Rossell: Good morning. I have been given the job of discussing an article that I published in *READ Perspectives* critiquing what has been known as the Collier study. In fact, it's co-authored by Wayne Thomas, and indeed he's the first author. This is a study that I first heard about three years ago, before the study had been completed, because Virginia Collier had been going around giving presentations on the findings of the study and then people would ask me to comment on it, and I would have to say, "I don't know, I can't comment on it. All I can tell you is that the study is not finished."

I found that in the ensuing years people would quote findings from the study, and since I knew the study was not out, I could say, "You haven't read it," and they would say, "How do you know?" I would say, "Because it isn't out."

The title of my article is, "Mystery on the Bilingual Express: A Critique of the Thomas and Collier Study." Perhaps no other yet-to-be-released report has been quoted so much or so often as the so-called Collier study. Not only has it been reported, but it has actually already influenced public policy, even before it was completed.

I know of at least two school districts that have implemented two-way bilingual programs because the Collier study, which they had not read, and which no one in their school district had read, said that kids in two-way bilingual programs did better than all other children.

Virginia Collier was holding public meetings in 1995, disseminating a five-page summary of her study, and that five-page summary consisted of two pages of text, two pages of line graphs, and a one-page list of program definitions.

Some two years later, the complete report has finally been issued. Although it is 96 pages long—and I printed out two copies of it last night from the Web—it contains no more data on the findings of the study than the same two charts in the original press release. There are several more graphs, but they are simply illustrations of the theories that are discussed. There are no tables in this study, and the report consists primarily of theories of bilingual education and criticism of the scientific method.

DESCRIPTION OF PROGRAM MODELS

The study analyzes eleven grades of achievement data over a fifteen-year period, from 1982 to 1996, in six elementary school programs for Limited-English Proficient children. The programs analyzed are:

Two-way bilingual education, a program in which children learn both English and Spanish, and the kids in the program are English monolingual speakers who want to learn Spanish and Spanish speakers who want to learn English.

The second program is a one-way developmental or maintenance bilingual program. Children are in this program to learn English, but also to maintain and to develop their Spanish.

The third type is transitional bilingual education with ESL taught through academic content. In this program, children are learning English and to the extent that they are taught in their native tongue, it is only as a means

Figure 1
Thomas and Collier's Chart of Elementary School Programs

PATTERNS OF K-12 ENGLISH LEARNERS' LONG-TERM
ACHIEVEMENT IN NCES ON STANDARDIZED TESTS IN ENGLISH
READING COMPARED ACROSS SIX PROGRAM MODELS
(Results aggregated from a series of 4–8 year longitudinal studies
from well-implemented, mature programs in five school districts)

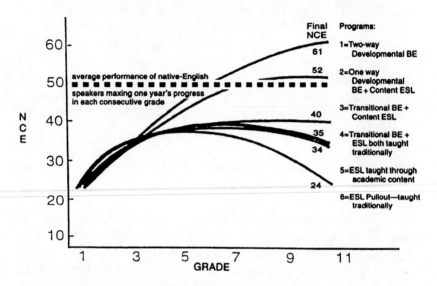

Source: From *School Effectiveness for Language Minority Students* (p. 53) by W. P. Thomas & V. Collier, December 1997, NCBE Resource Collection Series, No. 9. Washington, DC: National Clearing House for Bilingual Education. Copyright by Wayne P. Thomas and Virginia P. Collier, 1997. Reprinted with permission from NCBE and Thomas and Collier. http://www.ncbe.gwu.edu/ncbepubs/resource/effectiveness/thomas-collier97.pdf

ultimately to transition to English. The English that they learn is taught through academic content, and that means through subject matter. So they learn English while learning science and social studies, et cetera.

Transitional bilingual education taught traditionally is the fourth type of program. Although it isn't defined, I think "taught traditionally" means that the children are learning grammar and phonics, and that sort of thing.

The fifth program is ESL content, which is sometimes called sheltered or structured immersion, in which children are in an all-English environment, there's no native tongue instruction, but they're learning English as they're learning subject matter such as science and math and social studies.

Table 2

Reading Test Percentile Scores (Metropolitan) for Hispanic and White Students, Hernandez Two-Way Bilingual School, Boston, MA, May 1993

	GRADES							
	1	2	3	4	5	6	7	8
Hispanics Reading Score	—	—	—	43	30	30	25	39
Enrollment	*(26)*	*(26)*	*(25)*	*(25)*	*(22)*	*(19)*	*(10)*	*(15)*
Whites Reading Score	—	88	98	—	—	—	—	—
Enrollment	*(5)*	*(9)*	*(7)*	*(5)*	*(6)*	*(2)*	*(0)*	*(3)*

Key: —— means fewer than seven students took the test.

Source: Boston Public Schools (1994).

Table 3

Reading Test Scores (CAT 5) for Hispanic and White Students by Language Proficiency River Glenn Two-Way Bilingual School, San Jose, CA, Spring 1997

		Language Fluency Classification			
		LEP	FEP	English Only	TOTAL
Hispanics	Reading Score	20	41	33	
	Enrollment			*(150)*	*(283)*
Whites	Reading Score	—	—	65	
	Enrollment	*(0)*	*(0)*	*(113)*	*(113)*

Key: —— means fewer than seven students took the test.

Source: San Jose Unified School District (1998).

Table 4

Reading Test Scores in Grade Equivalents (CAT)
for Hispanic and White Students
Amigos Two-Way Bilingual Program,
Cambridge, MA, Spring 1991

		Grades		
		1	2	3
Hispanics	Reading Score	1.29	3.11	2.87
	(% Tested)	(46%)	(67%)	(47%)
Whites	Reading Score	1.30	5.09	4.70
	(% Tested)	(67%)	(100%)	(86%)

Source: Cazabon, Lambert, and Hall, (1991), p. 8, 14-16.

The sixth program is <u>ESL pullout</u>; that is, kids are in a regular classroom and they're pulled out for an English-as-a-Second-Language class for maybe one period a day, sometimes just three periods a week.

FINDINGS OF THOMAS AND COLLIER STUDY

The findings of the study are that students in the two-way bilingual education programs did the best, well above all the other programs. The second finding is that the one-way developmental bilingual programs did the second best; that is, if you develop your native tongue, ultimately you are going to be better in English. In the order that I spoke to them is the order of how well they did. So, two-way did best; one-way did second best; transitional bilingual education did the third best; transitional bilingual education taught traditionally did the fourth best; ESL content, fifth best; and the worst was ESL pullout.

The data that are shown in these line graphs (Figure 1 below), which are the only data in the Thomas and Collier Study, don't match the data found in scientific studies, or even in descriptive studies done in school districts around the U.S.

For example, in my article I show the results of the Cambridge, Massachusetts, Two-Way Amigos Program, the Boston Hernandez Program, and the San Jose, California, Two-Way Bilingual Program. The data in the Thomas and Collier Study on two-way bilingual programs is about 30 points higher than that in these other highly acclaimed bilingual education programs (see Tables 2, 3, and 4, below, reprinted from *READ Perspectives*, Vol. V-2, Fall 1998).

So there are many people who believe that the researchers have combined English-speaking scores and Spanish-speaking scores. Thomas and Collier, however, say they only have Spanish-speaking scores.

METHODOLOGICAL PROBLEMS WITH THOMAS AND COLLIER STUDY

One of the first problems with the study is that it is massive. It has 700,000 student records. Out of the 700,000 student records, they selected 42,317 with four years or more of data, and achievement growth with "some generalizability." They discarded results they thought were unique to a school district.

In essence, what they were doing is this: Of the 700,000 student records, they picked the data trends they thought were generalizable. If something was "unique"—and they don't describe what this means at all—Thomas and Collier threw it away.

So the point I make in my article is it's interesting how, with two more years of data, and the Ramirez study no longer being in it, the line graphs from the recent publication exactly match the line graphs from the 1995 study which had a whole lot less data. Now, how could that happen? The answer is, if you're picking only the achievement trends that you think are generalizable, anything that doesn't match your earlier line graphs, you don't use.

This is a large step backward in the efforts of social science to produce results that are not only generalizable but are *verifiable*. This study cannot be verified because none of us can ever know what they meant by generalizability.

The Thomas and Collier Study has several more serious problems. First, it uses a methodology that is a simple descriptive cohort analysis that is unscientific and that can produce misleading results. *The method is unscientific because each grade consists of different students.* Although 11 grades are studied, most students have only four years of achievement data, and there's no statistical control for pre-treatment differences that existed before the students were in the program.

The achievement of students enrolled in elementary school programs is compared to the achievement of different students in junior high and high school, who were apparently in similar programs in elementary school. So you've got different kids over time.

Now this is what school districts all over the country do. It's common, but it's wrong. In fact, I've often said that school districts are their own worst enemies, because they are constantly showing declining achievement, and I mathematically demonstrate in my published paper—I thought about doing an overhead, and then I decided if the peer reviewers thought that my analysis was too complex, I'm not going to be able to present it in an overhead—but the fact of the matter is that I mathematically demonstrate how each individual cohort of four years of data can have the exact opposite trend of the average summed-down grades.

This is why social scientists reject a descriptive cohort analysis. We don't use it because we know that it is mathematically possible to have averages that show the exact opposite of the pattern of each individual cohort. What I do is show how every kid in the two-way developmental bilingual program could have a decline in achievement, but the average shows an increase in achievement because you've got a four-year cohort over here, a four-year cohort there, and if they're the right cohorts, and if you're picking generalizable trends, you end up with a positive increase in achievement for the aggregate downgrades, even though every individual kid shows a decline.

I know this is difficult to understand, and it's particularly difficult to understand because school districts all over the country do this—they use this technique. They are wrong; they shouldn't do it; they are their own worst enemies.

By the way, another problem, just to comment on the first discussion, is in how we define English language learners. The definition of an English language learner is a low-achiever. If an English language learner, a kid from a language-minority background, scores above whatever criterion is used in the school district—right now I'm studying New York City, and it's the 40th percentile—the child is considered fluent English proficient. If you define a category by its low achievement, guess what? It's going to have low achievement. The reason why English language learners have low achievement is because that's how we define them.

The problem with all of this is that school districts are as confused as everybody else. But it's shocking to know that policy makers and policy analysts, who rely on research reports, are basing decisions on this so-called social science research study.

Even if Thomas and Collier had followed the same students over time, which they didn't do, this study would be unscientific because it is not possible to determine the effect of a program that a student participated in many years ago without controlling for the student's individual characteristics. There's no statistical control for the individual characteristics, i.e., pre-treatment differences.

If, for example, the kids in the two-way bilingual programs were of higher social class, then of course they're going to have higher achievement scores, but there's no control for that.

COMPLETE LACK OF DATA

Almost as disturbing as the methodological problems I've cited is the nearly complete lack of data in the study. Although it's 96 pages long, as I mentioned earlier, it contains no more data than the five-page 1995 press release. There's no information on any of the characteristics of any of these programs, the children enrolled in them, the schools or the school districts in which they reside.

We literally know nothing about these school districts and their schools, other than that there are five of them and they are moderate to large, urban and suburban school systems from all over the U.S. And even the programs are defined in generalities that could apply to any program of that type.

Whereas federal grant reports typically have dozens of tables, charts, and appendices on the characteristics of the sample, methodology, and statistical analysis representing one-half to two-thirds of the report, the Thomas and Collier report has only two line graphs on the findings of the study representing 1 percent of the report.

I consider this a new low in federal grant reporting. I was simply stunned by the lack of data, and it makes me wonder what is going on in the federal government, because my last federal grant report not only had two-thirds of the report, which was huge, filled with tables and data on everything, including the methodologies, statistical analysis, et cetera, et cetera, but we had to rewrite and rewrite because they wanted more data, and they wanted the data explained. We went through a period of six months of rewriting to produce additional tables.

CONCLUSION

I can honestly say that in twenty-five years of reading technical reports, I've never seen a federally funded empirical research study with so little information in it. But I have also never seen a study—and this I find just quite stunning—where the researchers are as honest as they are; indeed, they brag about it, about the fact that they have transcended the problems with the scientific method and they are going to kick trends they think are not generalizable, and this they consider to be a step forward in research.

I consider it to be a huge step backward, and I can honestly tell you that you cannot rely on the Collier Study for any generalizations about any programs, and I think the title of my article, "Mystery on the Bilingual Express," accurately describes the problem with this study. As Lee Porter said in something I read, there simply is no beef there, there's no data for the reader.

Thank you.

—

(Editor's Note: "Mystery on the Bilingual Express: A Critique of the Thomas and Collier Study," was published in its entirety in *READ Perspectives*, Vol. V-2, Fall 1998. The Executive Summary is reprinted at the end of the conference papers, page 117, as Appendix 1.)

EL PASO PROGRAMS FOR ENGLISH LANGUAGE LEARNERS: A FOLLOW-UP STUDY

Charles Glenn: Rosalie Porter, the dynamo who brought us here today and is our next speaker, is herself an English language learner, then a Spanish/English bilingual teacher, and for a decade the bilingual program director in Newton, Massachusetts. I first heard of her when I was in charge of urban education and civil rights for the Massachusetts Department of Education and everyone was complaining about the rebel in Newton, but I have always had a liking for rebels.

Rosalie Porter: We had hoped that Professor Russell Gersten of the University of Oregon would be here to report on his findings, but he is speaking at this very moment at a conference in Miami. In his place, I will present the main conclusions of the two studies he conducted for the READ Institute. Gersten analyzed and reported on the comparative second language acquisition and academic achievement of limited-English students in two different programs in the El Paso, Texas, Independent School District.

The El Paso study that the READ Institute commissioned in 1992 was our very first piece of research on a school district's bilingual programs. The elements of good education research were followed: Students in both the control group and the treatment group had the same characteristics, i.e., all were non-English speakers, or very limited English speakers, when they began school; all are of Mexican American background; all are from the same socioeconomic background; and all are attending schools in the same district. The 228 students in the original study were enrolled in two very different instructional programs. El Paso had started its Spanish transitional bilingual education program in 1970. After a number of years, an experimental model called the "Bilingual Immersion Project" was initiated under the direction of then Assistant Superintendent, Rosita Apodaca. The control group contained students in five transitional bilingual education program schools and the treatment group was made up of students in five bilingual immersion model schools. The comparison between these two groups of students was monitored over a period of 10 years.

The two programs differed quite dramatically. The transitional bilingual program provides instruction in reading, writing, and school subjects in Spanish for the first three or four years, with approximately 30 to 60 minutes of English teaching per day. The bilingual immersion program instead delivers all instruction in literacy and subject matter through a special English language program, with 30 to 90 minutes a day of Spanish. You could almost say they were a mirror image of each other.

Because of the difference in the proportions of English language usage in the two programs, students in the transitional bilingual program were not tested in English until fourth grade. In grade 4, both groups of students were tested with the Iowa Test of Basic Skills (ITBS), an assessment instrument which is used in many school districts. Test scores reported in language, reading, and math favored the bilingual immersion students in each of these subjects. If the rate of exit from a special program is a fair measure of success, then the immersion students prevailed decisively in this area. At the end of fifth grade, 99 percent of the immersion students were in mainstream classrooms, doing their schoolwork in English without special help, while even by the seventh grade one-third of the control group students were still in the bilingual program.

Teachers were surveyed for their attitudes toward the two programs. As is often the case when you start a new program and train teachers to do new things, there was a more positive attitude toward the immersion program. A majority of teachers said that students were learning English more rapidly and effectively in the immersion classrooms than in the bilingual classrooms.

Interviews with students revealed that all of the students had the same level of self-esteem. In other words, the students who were taught in English from the first day of school had not suffered a loss of self-esteem, nor did they show any signs of greater stress from being taught in a second language.

Thus, the differences between these two programs in the first four or five years of schooling are substantial, since the study found that the English immersion students learned their school subjects and learned to speak, read, and write in English at a faster pace. It took two to three years longer for the bilingual program students to reach the same levels of achievement as the immersion students, but by the end of seventh grade, it is reasonable to say that both programs achieved the same goals.

In 1996, the READ Institute commissioned a follow-up study by Professor Gersten. Data were collected on students from the original study who were still in the El Paso schools—now in 10th, 11th, and 12th grades. Student test scores on the Texas Assessment of Academic Skills (TAAS), the statewide test required for high school graduation, were the measure of achievement. All students are expected to take the TAAS in 10th grade. Students who are not successful in passing the test of reading, writing, and mathematics on their first try are given special tutoring and may retake the test several more times until they score a passing grade. Here, there is rather discouraging news.

All of the students (of the original 228 there were 176 still in the district who had all started school together in first grade) performed at about the same level, whether they had been in the Spanish bilingual program or the English immersion program. Unfortunately, that level is not very high. A majority of the students were able to pass the graduation test at the very lowest level, so they were able to graduate

Figure 1

Status Dropout Rates

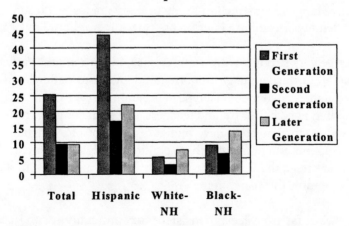

Source: Departments of Education and CPS, October 1996. Status dropout rate is percent of individuals 16 to 24 who were not enrolled in school and had not completed high school.

from high school. There was no statistically significant difference in the academic performance of students in the two groups, not only on the TAAS test, but also in their grade point averages which were about the same. Another troubling factor reported by this study is the high rate of high school dropouts before completing high school: 26.5 percent for students who had been in bilingual classrooms; 19.5 percent for the immersion program students. I am informed that the difference between the two is not statistically significant but at least to me this small difference proves once again that there need not be harmful effects from the early learning of English as a second language in a school setting.

What conclusions can we draw from this study? We can say with certainty that English language and literacy and subject-matter learning can be achieved as well in an intensive English program as in a bilingual (native language instruction) program. It takes a few years longer in a bilingual program. We can say that if there is a value in having bilingual students integrated in regular classrooms at a more rapid pace, then there is some advantage for the immersion program.

There was not a higher level of performance by either group after 10 to 12 years of schooling. It would appear to me that the predictions of bilingual education advocates—principally Jim Cummins, Steve Krashen, David Ramirez, and Virginia Collier—that several years of native language instruction in the primary grades will result in better academic performance later on are certainly not borne out.

I agree very strongly with Diane August, in her remarks earlier today, that all of our language-minority students need better learning opportunities, no matter what type of program they are involved in. These children need better-trained teachers, more challenging curricula and texts. Teachers need to have higher expectations for language minority students and must hold these children to higher standards. School districts need the flexibility to be creative and innovative in the range of programs they can offer.

Last, but far from least, consistent accountability for the academic progress of language minority students is long overdue. Bilingual children need to be tested along with their English-speaking classmates, after one, two, or three years in U.S. schools. Whatever rule is established in each district, universal assessment of student development is the only effective way to determine what improvements are needed.

(Editor's Note: "El Paso Programs for English Language Learners: A Follow-Up Study,"by Professors Russell Gersten, Scott Baker and Thomas Keating of the Eugene Research Institute at the University of Oregon, was published in its entirety in *READ Perspectives,* Vol. V-1, Spring 1998. The Executive Summary of the study is reprinted at the end of the conference papers as Appendix 2, page 120.)

LABOR MARKET EFFECTS OF BILINGUAL EDUCATION AMONG HISPANIC WORKERS

Charles Glenn: We're particularly interested to have Mark Lopez here today because one of the weaknesses of education research in general is that not much of it is genuinely longitudinal; that is, we don't really learn what happens to kids over time, which after all is the fundamental issue in education.

Mark, who is assistant professor at the University of Maryland, is an economist. He conducts research on various issues involving what affects the achievement and participation in our society of language-minority children and adults. So we will be looking beyond immediate program effects to what the long-term effects are of the kind of education we provide to kids.

Mark Lopez: Good morning, I hope everybody's doing well. Today, I'd like to talk about the labor market effects of bilingual education among Hispanic workers. This is a study that a colleague of mine, Marie Mora, and I have done together. We were interested in looking at the long-range effects of bilingual education for a couple of reasons.

First, we know that there is an English proficiency gap. In the United States today, large and growing numbers of non-English speakers are in the workforce, and that has implications for the labor market. Those implications in particular are the following: There is an English proficiency penalty that one pays if one does not speak English very well, and one pays that penalty through lower wages and through lower

Table 1

Regression Adjusted Earnings Differences Between Bilingual Education Participants and Non-Participants by Immigrant Status
Hispanics Only
(weighted differences)

	Bilingual Education Participants	Bilingual Education Non-Participants	Approximate % Difference
Immigrants N=216	$18,478	$24,200	−31%**
Second Generation N=253	$18,886	$23,513	−24.5%**
Third Generation N=645	$17,292	$17,516	−1.3%
Full Sample N=1,298	$17,294	$17,040	1.0%

occupational attainment; this is fairly well documented in the economics literature. What do we know about Hispanics? Currently, for Hispanic workers, the wage gap is at about 20 percent to 30 percent; that is, Hispanic workers earn about 20 percent to 30 percent of what their white counterparts earn, and the gap can be explained by two very important factors:

The first is that Hispanics generally tend to get little formal education. This can be seen in the graph of status dropout rates (see Figure 1).

As economists, we have funny definitions for different types of dropout rates. Status dropout rates refer to the proportion of all individuals who have not completed a high school diploma, who are currently not enrolled in school, and who are between the ages of 16 and 24. These data are drawn from the 1996 Current Population Survey, so it's pretty recent. What you can see in the graph is that among Hispanics, the dropout rate is fairly high and, I may add, it has not improved in a dozen years. However, the fact of low educational attainment goes a long way toward explaining the reason why Hispanics actually earn less than non-Hispanics.

Table 2

Regression Adjusted Earnings Differences Between ESL, Transitional Bilingual Education (TBE) Participants and Non-Participants by Immigrant Status: Hispanic Workers in *HSB*.

	Full Sample	First Generation	Second Generation	Third or More Generation
	(1)	(2)	(3)	(4)
ESL	$17,212	$19,674	$21,712	$14,012
TBE	17,041	17,664	18,227	19,462
No bilingual education	17,040	24,200	23,513	17,516
Approximate Difference	*	*	*	
ESL vs. No BE	1%	−23%	−8.3%	−25%
TBE vs. No BE	0.01%	−37%	−29%	10%
TBE vs. ESL	−1%	−11%	−19%	28%
Number of observations	1,298	216	253	645

* Statistically significant at the 1 percent and 5 percent level.

Source: Restricted-Use High School and Beyond (HSB) base year (1980), first follow-up (1982), and fourth follow-up (1992) surveys. See text for sample restrictions and at-risk definition used in this study.[1]

The second reason that explains the earnings gap for Hispanics is lack of English language proficiency. When one controls for these two factors, the Hispanic wage gap is actually eliminated. This clearly suggests some policy prescriptions: first, trying to keep Hispanic students in school, that's extremely important; but, second, that something like bilingual education might be an appropriate policy to pursue if it actually improves English proficiency.

That was our initial motivation for actually looking at these particular data. So what Marie and I did was to look at a longitudinal data set that actually has some bilingual education information in it. The data set we looked at was a study done by the U.S. Department of Educa-

Table 3

Occupational Distribution of "At Risk" Hispanic Workers in the Restricted-Use HSB Data Files Across Bilingual Education Participants and Non-Participants.

Occupation	Non-Participants	Bilingual Education Participants
Clerical	0.187	0.153
Craftsman	0.032	0.047
Farmer	0.000	0.001
Laborer	0.139	0.201
Management	0.161	0.136
Military	0.023	0.010
Skilled Operative	0.033	0.065
Professional	0.088	0.082
Owner of a Business	0.018	0.013
Protective Services	0.025	0.029
Sales	0.076	0.052
Teaching	0.018	0.010
Service	0.060	0.059
Technical	0.024	0.025
Number of Observations	827	471

Source: Authors' tabulations from the Restricted-Use High School and Beyond (HSB) fourth follow-up. See text for sample restrictions and "at-risk" definition used in this study.[2]

tion called *High School and Beyond*. It was conducted in 1980, initially, so it's actually getting a little bit old, but in 1980, the students who were interviewed were sophomores in high school. They were again followed up in 1992, ten years after high school, and were asked several questions about educational attainment, labor market earnings, occupational distributions, and so forth.

From the data, we were able to define bilingual education in a couple of ways. The first definition is broad; essentially it includes any sort of special language assistance. We then divided that first definition into two components—English as a Second Language (ESL) and Transitional Bilingual Education (TBE).

Generally speaking, ESL is any sort of special language instruction in English that does not use the native language for any classroom instruction. Transitional Bilingual Education usually includes some measure of native language instruction, with the addition of ESL lessons. At least that's the way we're able to construct these variables from the data.

The data show that among those students in our sample who are considered bilingual education participants, about 69 percent went through Transitional Bilingual Education, and about 31 percent were in ESL programs. These proportions match some of the national data we see, but it does seem as though the number of participants overall is relatively low.

Now, our sample of analysis contains only Hispanics, and we attempted to mimic the selection process in identifying potential candidates for bilingual education in this data by mimicking the process that states actually use to select students. Thus, we used the home language survey process. We don't have English proficiency test scores, so we're a little bit off on that. But, together, this produces a sample of about 1,200 students, of which 471 are participating in some sort of program.

Our sample characteristics, to give some background here, are the following: Relative to non-participants, we find the bilingual education participants are more likely to be immigrants, predominantly from lower socioeconomic households, and they tend to score lower on academic tests.

All this matches data we see in other studies. Hispanic students enrolled in bilingual programs are those students who have been identified as Limited-English Proficient and often times are also students who are having academic difficulties and are scoring low on proficiency exams.

Now, what did our findings show? Here's the first set of results. These are adjusted earnings (see Table 1, below). We have controlled for the family background of students and for the school characteristics of the schools the students attended, and we have a lot of data on that.

These results, as you can see, suggest the following: First, if we just look at the full sample, there appears to be no difference. However, when we start looking at first generation (immigrant children) and second generation (the children of immigrant parents) separately, we begin to see some differences. Those students who actually went through bilingual programs are doing worse in the labor market 10 years after high school than those who did not receive native language instruction. Some of these differences are on the order of 25 percent to 33 percent lower earnings, as shown in Table 1.

For the first generation figures, the bilingual education students were earning approximately $18,500 in 1991, and the non-participants in bilingual education were earning about $24,200. This illustrates how big a gap we're talking about here.

We also wanted to examine differences by program type because there's more to it than just simply generalizing about bilingual education. By program type here's what we found. When we observe the full sample results, there appear to be no differences between ESL, TBE, and no bilingual education (see Table 2). But among the first generation students, if we look at ESL versus Transitional Bilingual Education, we see a difference. Again, we see a difference in the second-generation data, i.e., ESL appears to produce better results than transitional bilingual education.

In third generation students, we have a flip that we were unable to explain. It seems more than a little strange that a large number of third generation students are still participating in language assistance programs. However, this is a fact we are unable to explain.

We also looked at occupational distribution (Table 3), which reveals the troubling information that students formerly in bilingual education programs are generally in lower-paying jobs. While school program participation does not explain the whole difference in earnings, it does partly explain the difference.

What sort of conclusions do we draw from these particular data? One, that bilingual education participants, in the long run, earn no more or less on average than their peers who participated in English immersion programs. However, the more recent a student's immigration, the worse off the bilingual program participants appear to be; that is, their earnings tend to be less. This is particularly true for first- and second-generation students, who exhibit substantial differences in labor market earnings between TBE and ESL. On occupational attainment, we also see that bilingual program participants are concentrated in lower-paying occupations than those who had been in ESL.

What does it all mean? This is part of a larger set of work that my co-author and I are engaged in, looking at long-term effects. What we generally find is that in the long run, students who have reported being in bilingual programs are actually earning less, completing fewer years of formal schooling, not going on to higher education or earning college degrees, and dropping out of high school in greater numbers than those students of similar backgrounds who didn't go through these programs.

Since we completed this preliminary study, we have done subsequent work in order to make sure that our sample of analysis is appropriate and to make certain that we have a good comparison group with which to draw conclusions. The results I have reported today actually continue to hold. The main conclusion appears to be that Limited-English Proficient students who participate in bilingual programs, when compared to a similar set of students who do not, are found to be achieving less in labor market earnings and in quality of occupations attained, in the long run.

NOTES

1. The above models are estimated using OLS with the log of average earnings in 1990 and 1991 as the dependent variable. The above figures (in dollars) are weighted using HSB's fourth follow-up cross-sectional weight. The "Third or More" immigration generation column includes individuals classified as "second/third" in Table 1. See text for a discussion of the construction of the bilingual education participation variable. Other controls include jobmarket experience (in months) and experience-squared, personal variables (marital status, gender, years of education, region and urban status of high school, 1980 family income level as five binary variables, parental education level as ten binary variables, and home ownership in 1980, categorical variables for immigrant generation and years since arrival), 1980 high school general characteristics (racial composition of the high school, starting teacher's salary, per pupil district expenditures, the pupil/

teacher ratio, and whether the school is private); and a set of academic characteristics representing the 1980 academic achievement quartile. The average age of sample members is 28. Individual immigrant generation groupings do not sum to the full sample number of observations since we are unable to identify immigrant status for all sample members.

2. Categories do not sum to 1.00 because of rounding errors and missing data. All results are weighted using the fourth follow-up cross-sectional weight.

PANEL II - PRACTITIONERS: SUCCESSFUL PROGRAMS AND NEW APPROACHES

Moderator, Rosalie Pedalino Porter, READ Institute

Rosalie Porter: The organizing principle for this panel was to bring together educators representing three distinctly different programs: a transitional bilingual education program in a large urban district; a two-way Program; and an English immersion Program. In addition, Professor Maria Brisk of Boston University was invited to contribute her views on the most essential elements of effective schooling for limited-English students.

We invited the director in charge of the Transitional Bilingual Education program in the Lowell, Massachusetts, Public Schools, a large urban district that recently went through a thorough evaluation of its program and is instituting improvements. Unfortunately, the Lowell speaker withdrew just a few days ago.

We invited the coordinator of the Two-Way *Amigos* Program in the Cambridge, Massachusetts, Public School. This program has been in existence for twelve years and has a track record of student achievement.

And we invited the superintendent of the Bethlehem Public Schools in Pennsylvania to describe their English Acquisition Program, now in its fifth year and beginning to report consistent improvements in second-language learning.

Our first presenter on this panel is Mary Cazabon, who has been involved in bilingual and ESL programs in Cambridge for twenty years. She has pioneered work in this state in developing inclusive programs that bring together elementary school children of many different language backgrounds with English speakers, educating the children in two languages.

REFLECTIONS OF A BILINGUAL EDUCATOR: FROM PAST TO PRESENT

Mary T. Cazabon:

Almost Twenty-five Years Ago

As a first year teacher, I remember the frustration I felt about my bilingual students' isolation from the rest of the students in the school. I worried about their need for socialization with peers and their exposure to high-quality curriculum. As a novice English as a Second Language (ESL) teacher, I was responsible for delivering instruction in all content subjects to students ranging from 10 to 15 years old in a self-contained, transitional bilingual education classroom. Even with the support from my students' Spanish and Chinese native-language teachers, I was faced with an overwhelming challenge. I knew that my students could learn from their English-speaking peers, and that as a fledgling teacher, I had much to learn from my colleagues, but the opportunities for student-to-student or teacher-to-teacher interactions did not exist. I believed in bilingual education, but I wanted more for my students.

During my first years of teaching, I embarked on a personal crusade to find ways to integrate my students with mainstream children and ways for me to work with the monolingual English curriculum teachers. As a result, I collaborated with my more experienced colleagues, and we began to exchange students for specialized group projects and to integrate students in language arts, math, and social studies classes.

When I became an administrator of bilingual education programs, I wanted to formalize and extend to all schools and programs what I had learned to be good teaching practice—the integration of bilingual and mainstream students. In order to improve education for language-minority students, bilingual program directors cannot work alone. They must be proactive members of the school department's administrative team and engage everyone in the discussion of bilingual program development. I have found that collaboration and collective problem-solving with school personnel around issues affecting our English language learners are the important ways to ensure that all students are challenged to attain high standards. *Amigos*, our first two-way bilingual immersion program, was the result of just such a collaborative effort.

Amigos Two-Way Spanish/ English Language Immersion Program

Amigos is our longest implemented, integrated bilingual education program and the one for which we have conducted longitudinal research. *Amigos* is a two-way immersion program that educators instituted in Cambridge, Massachusetts, in 1986 (see Cazabon, Lambert & Hall, 1993; Lambert & Cazabon, 1994, Cazabon, Nicoladis & Lambert, 1998). Half of each class is composed of native English speakers and half native Spanish speakers. Native language speaking teachers (one Spanish- and one English-speaking) conduct half the instruction time in Spanish and half in English. There are two classrooms of students per grade level from kindergarten through grade 8.

Students are never separated for instruction. Two-way programs differ from immersion bilingual education and Transitional Bilingual Education programs on the dimension of student integration. Mixing students racially and linguistically is not a goal of immersion bilingual education programs (see Baker, 1996) or of Transitional Bilingual Education (see Massachusetts General Laws, Chapter 71A). In both instances students are primarily monolingual speakers: majority-language speakers in the former and minority- language speakers in the latter.

Yearly Evaluations

In the Cambridge schools, we have evaluated students' progress since the inception of *Amigos*. Wallace E. Lambert has served as principal program evaluator since 1986. The three major goals of the *Amigos* program are:

1. Students' high-level academic and language development in English and in Spanish;
2. Students' cultivation of cross-cultural friendships and increased knowledge about their own cultural distinctiveness; and
3. Involvement of parents in their childrens' education.

Respective to the attainment of program goals, Lambert has consistently found that students in the *Amigos* program are moving toward a state of balanced bilingualism in their oral language and academic development. They also appear to be moving toward biculturality. Instruction in Spanish has not set them back in terms of their English

Table 1

Students' Self-Report of Competence
SECOND GRADE
End of the School Year, 1997-98

1. How good are you at the following subjects?
   (1=Poor; 2=Not Bad; 3=Good; 4=Very Good)

	English Amigos (n=12)	Spanish Amigos (n=17)
a) Spanish reading	3.17 (0.58)	3.53 (0.72)
b) Spanish math	3.83 (0.39)	3.18 (0.64)
c) English reading	3.83 (0.39)	3.29 (0.99)
d) English math	3.83 (0.39)	3.42 (0.87)

2. How much do you like the following subjects?
   (1=Not at all; 2=Not Much; 3=Some; 4=A Lot)

	English *Amigos* (n=12)	Spanish *Amigos* (n=17)
a) Spanish reading	3.25 (0.97)	3.47 (0.72)
b) Spanish math	3.67 (0.78)	3.47 (0.62)
c) English reading	3.50 (0.67)	3.65 (0.49)
d) English math	4.00 (0.00)	3.33 (0.80)

academic attainment. Lambert has also found an increase in parental involvement at the school level.

For the assessment of English language achievement, we use the CAT (California Achievement Test, CTB McGraw Hill, 1985), a nationwide measure of grade level standing. All *Amigos* students in grades 2 through 8 take the reading and math sub-tests. Until 1995–96, we used the SABE (Spanish Achievement in Bilingual Education, CTB McGraw Hill, 1991) to measure Spanish language achievement in reading and math; and from 1996 until now, we have been using the SUPERA (Spanish language version of Terra Nova, CTB McGraw Hill, 1997).

We also use a variety of other assessment measures, including English and Spanish writing samples, the Language Assessment Scales: Reading and Writing (CTB McGraw Hill, 1994) and oral language dominance testing in both languages. We also administer attitudinal questionnaires concerning students' cross-cultural attitudes, teachers' judgment of student competence, students' perceived competence of themselves, and students' self-report of competence.

By way of illustration, I offer Table 1 (Students' Self-Report of Competence for Second Grade Based on End of the School Year, 1997–1998), which summarizes the students' collective responses divided by English *Amigos* (English home-speakers) and Spanish *Amigos* (Spanish home-speakers). For this questionnaire, I present the averages and standard deviations for the results. No tests of statistical difference were performed on these data, because there were no comparable control groups available who were studying in both Spanish and English. Table 1 summarizes how the two groups of students answered two questions: (1) How good are you at the following subjects? and (2) How much do you like the following subjects? Responses targeted Spanish reading, Spanish math, English reading, and English math.

Response to question 1: How good are you at the following subjects?

Using a Likert-type 4 point scale, students indicated "how good they were" by choosing numerical responses ranging from (1) poor, (2) not bad, (3) good, to (4) very good. In general, both English and Spanish second grade *Amigos* students felt they were "good" in all subjects in English and Spanish. Overall, the English *Amigos* rated being close to 4 "very good" with a score of 3.83 in three subjects: Spanish math, English reading, and English math. The Spanish *Amigos* felt they were best in Spanish reading (3.53) followed closely by English math (3.42).

Response to question 2: How much do you like the following subjects?

Using a Likert-type 4 point scale, students indicated "how much they liked" each subject by choosing numerical responses ranging from (1) not at all, (2) not much, (3) some, to (4) a lot. Both groups indicated liking all the subjects more than 3, "some," and close to 4, "a lot." The English *Amigos* liked English math (4.00) the most, followed by Spanish math (3.67). The Spanish *Amigos* liked English reading (3.65) the most, followed by Spanish reading (3.47) and Spanish math (3.47).

A LONGITUDINAL LOOK AT STANDARDIZED TESTS ADMINISTERED TO *AMIGOS* PROGRAM STUDENTS: 1990–91 THROUGH 1996–97

Our usual way of reporting on the *Amigos* program is to present yearly results from reading and mathematics scores in English and Spanish

Table 2

Summary of Comparison
Between the *Amigos* Groups and the English Controls on the CAT (California Achievement Test)

English-*Amigos* vs. English Controls

	Reading	Math
Grade 4	EA (n=75) above controls (n=78)	EA (n=75) above controls (n=70)
Grade 5	EA (n=53) above controls (n=75)	EA (n=51) above controls (n=75)
Grade 6	EA (n=24) above controls (n=10)	EA (n=24) above controls (n=10)
Grade 7	EA (n=12) above controls (n=7)	No difference EA (n=12); Controls (n=7)
Grade 8	EA (n=11) above controls (n=42)	EA (n=11) above controls (n=44)

Spanish *Amigos* vs. English Controls

	Reading	Math
Grade 4	SA (n=108) above controls (n=78)	SA (n=108) above controls (n=70)
Grade 5	SA (n=83) above controls (n=75)	SA (n=88) above controls (n=75)
Grade 6	SA (n=25) above controls (n=10)	SA (n=25) above controls (n=10)
Grade 7	SA (n=18) above controls (n=7)	SA (n=19) above controls (n=7)
Grade 8	SA (n=16) above controls(n=42)	No difference SA (n=15); Controls (n=44)

Note: EA = English *Amigos*; SA = Spanish *Amigos*

on standardized tests. We normally have two classes in the earlier grades and one or two classes in grades 7 and 8, with each class averaging about 20 students. When we break a class down into ethnic subgroups, we are usually dealing with 10 to 12 Spanish *Amigos*, and

8 to 10 English *Amigos* who are either "majority" (white) or "minority" (usually African-American) students. We combined the test results over seven years from 1990–91 through 1996–97 in order to enhance the total numbers for each breakdown group to provide a better perspective on student progress in the overall program. (For more complete, detailed information, see Cazabon et al., 1998.) The results in Spanish reflect only six years, because during the seventh year, 1996–97, we participated in a norming study for a new Spanish test, the *Supera*, and no test results were made available due to the pilot testing.

All students were administered the Coloured Progressive Matrices (Raven, 1986). Scores provide an index of each student's non-verbal intelligence or abstract reasoning ability. The students' scores were co-varied on the achievement tests using their scores on the Raven test. Therefore, we compare *Amigos* students and control-group students who share similar ability in non-verbal and abstract reasoning. We also note that in our comparisons all students have similar socio-economic backgrounds.

The results of our seven-year longitudinal study (Cazabon et al., 1998) from 1990 through 1997 indicate that the *Amigos* students are not losing ground academically in either math or reading in English and Spanish. The data from these analyses of seven years of the *Amigos* program suggest that both the English *Amigos* and Spanish *Amigos* are acquiring reading skills in both English and Spanish and are using the two languages to solve math problems (p. 12). Table 2 summarizes the comparisons of CAT results between English *Amigos* vs. English Controls as well as Spanish *Amigos* vs. English Controls.

NEW DIRECTIONS FOR CAMBRIDGE IN BILINGUAL EDUCATION

In Massachusetts, the passage of the Massachusetts Educational Reform Act of 1993 opened the door to collaborative and reciprocal opportunities between world language specialists and bilingual educators. The new Massachusetts World Language Curricular Frameworks require all children in the Commonwealth to begin a world language at the kindergarten level and to continue world language study through grade 12. Uniting the worlds of bilingual education and world language instruction is an exciting way for students whose first language is not English to learn together with students who need to acquire a second language. An alliance between the two programs offers a unique opportunity for cross-language fertilization and a chance for students to learn each other's languages in an integrated setting.

In Cambridge, we have undertaken a reform movement in all of our Transitional Bilingual Education programs. Our *perestroika* began with the opening of our bilingual programs to all students in the school. Through the promotion of the language-minority students' language as the world language for all children in the school, all children learn together. We also wanted to ensure two things: that our bilingual and monolingual students would all receive high-quality instruction, and that our curriculum would be aligned with the Massachusetts Department of Education Curriculum Frameworks.

A Title VII systemwide, five-year bilingual education reform grant has enabled us to provide intensive staff training and engage in curriculum development. This effort has promoted extensive collaboration among teaching colleagues and an exploration of multiple ways to communicate with parents. We are not only improving native language instruction for bilingual students, but we are also offering innovative, shared second language instruction for English home speaking students. Now in the fourth year of the grant, we are providing integrated language instruction for native and non-native speakers in Mandarin, Portuguese, Spanish, French, and Korean to students at six elementary schools. We have also aligned our own World Language Developmental Curricula with the Massachusetts World Language Frameworks.

I have worked in the field of bilingual education for nearly a quarter of a century—interrupting my tour of duty only for a six-week period to give birth to my youngest daughter. My own three daughters have all participated in some form of bilingual education. My oldest daughter attended an Armenian bilingual program as a high school student. My middle child spent her kindergarten year in the Spanish transitional bilingual program in Cambridge, and my youngest spent eight years in the *Amigos* program. As the older two finish their graduate studies, they concur that their knowledge of more than one language has been an asset to them in many ways. It has been a skill that they could bring forth not only in securing employment opportunities, but it has also helped them to achieve a broader understanding of the world. Isn't that what we want for all students?

REFERENCES

Baker, C. (1996). *Foundations of bilingual education*. (2nd ed.) Clevedon, England: Multilingual Matters, Ltd.

Cazabon, M., Lambert, W., & Hall, G. (1993). *Two-way bilingual education: A progress report on the amigos program*. Santa Cruz, CA: National Center for Research on Cultural Diversity and Second Language Learning.

Cazabon, M., Nicoladis, E., & Lambert, W. E. (1998). *Becoming bilingual in the amigos two-way immersion program*. Santa Cruz, CA: National Center for Research on Cultural Diversity and Second Language Learning.

Lambert, W. E. & Cazabon, M. (1994). *Students' views of the amigos program*. Santa Cruz, CA: National Center for Research on Cultural Diversity and Second   Language Learning.

Massachusetts General Laws, Bilingual Law, Chapter 71A. MA (1971).

Recommended Readings on Two-Way Programs

Christian, D., Montone, C.L., Lindholm, K.J., & Carranza, I. (1997). *Profiles in two-way immersion education*. Washington, DC: Center for Applied Linguistics and Delta Systems Co.

Lindholm, K. (1990). Bilingual immersion in education: criteria for program development. In A. Padilla, H. Fairchild & C.Valdéz (Eds.), *Bilingual education issues and strategies*. Newbury Park, CA: Sage.

Rhodes, N. C., Christian, D., & Barfield, S. (1997). Innovations in immersion: The Key School two-way model. In R. K. Johnson, & M. Swain.(Eds.), *Immersion education: International perspectives* (pp. 265-283). Cambridge, U.K.: Cambridge University Press.

BETHLEHEM, PENNSYLVANIA'S ENGLISH ACQUISITION PROGRAM

Rosalie Porter: Dr. Thomas Doluisio is the superintendent of the Bethlehem Area School District in Pennsylvania. He is an experienced educator with a background in high school teaching and some years of service as a high school principal. He led his school district in developing a new approach in educating the district's language-minority students, which started in 1993.

Thomas J. Doluisio: I was invited to give you some background on the decision to change the Bethlehem program for limited-English students from a Spanish bilingual program to an English acquisition approach and to give a brief description of the new program and the results we are seeing. I title my presentation, "The Demise of Bilingual Education in the Bethlehem Area School District."

Let me begin by telling you about the Bethlehem Area School District. We are the sixth largest school district out of 501 in the Commonwealth. We have 14,000 students with in our school district. About 24 percent are Latinos. There are approximately 70 percent white students and about 5 percent "other."

Our Latino students look something like this: Many are poor, many come from single-parent homes. These students are highly mobile, and usually their parents are intimidated by the bureaucracy represented by a public school system. I know that these parents care very much about their children. They just do not yet know how to access the power, and very frankly, they are very trusting of teachers and principals. These Latino parents trust that just about anything we do for and with their children is the right thing. The power of schools to determine what policies are best for special populations such as language-minority children—with little fear of being challenged by the trusting parents—carries with it the danger that ineffective programs may be initiated and maintained.

What brought us to the point in 1993 of eliminating the bilingual education program? Simply stated, I became very frustrated. It came to a head when I realized that because of the language barrier, it was taking seven to eight years to mainstream Latino students into regular school programs. That had detrimental effects on their ability to socialize and assimilate into the overall school population. It also reinforced a lot of biases in our community and within our student body. We were segregating our Latino students within our school district. Students sat at opposite ends of the cafeteria. They just were not talking to one another, and this carried over into other areas of school and community life and caused problems.

Very few Latinos were in the college preparatory programs in our two high schools. In addition, very few were getting into higher education programs. The local community college reported that because of the language barrier with our Latino students, it needed to establish remedial programs and teach the students English before they could be placed into freshman-level courses. Quite frankly, that irritated and frustrated me because I was looking at myself and saying, "Hey, Doluisio, you are the guy who can do something about that."

I very much respect our administrators who are advocates of bilingual programs, although I did not necessarily agree with them. I believed that many were operating with their hearts, but I felt we needed to approach education with our heads. We were "user-friendly"—very warm and fuzzy—and had Latino children segregated for seven to eight years with very few getting into college or being prepared for the working world.

There were other philosophical differences between the bilingual education advocates and me, besides the seven to eight years it was taking to fully mainstream Latinos. We have to prepare these young people to meet high academic standards, make them job and marketplace competitive, and ready for the challenges of the twenty-first century. Quite frankly, I do not feel we should spend valuable instructional time maintaining culture; that's the job of the parents.

Another area of disagreement I had with the staff members who were managing our bilingual programs in Bethlehem was that they were spending precious instructional time teaching our students to feel good about themselves. I believe that if we teach them English and these students succeed in school, get high grades, are competitive, go to college, and get good jobs after high school, they will indeed feel good about themselves. I do not believe that second-grade students who are poor readers, cannot speak English, and do not have a clue as to what is going on in their classroom, should be taught to feel good about themselves.

So, there was a big philosophical chasm between our program staff and me. What did I do about this? I created a committee, what else! I put together a committee of administrators, teachers, and parents in our school district. Six months later the committee brought forward a report which basically said—maintain the status quo! I then put out my own report, a minority report if you will, opposing the committee recommendation. I took their report and mine to the community and said, "Let's have a discussion." We had public hearings in front of our school board, and the auditorium was filled for several evenings. We had people on opposite sides of the issue sitting on opposite sides of the aisle, and there was also a smattering of racism and ignorance expressed at the hearings. So, we had a community debate over a two-month period. I think it brought out the best and worst in people in our community. Fortunately, a lot of professional Latinos came forward—doctors, lawyers, and educators—who said, "You need to teach young Latinos to speak English as soon as possible." Their support was comforting and very important to me. They had credibility because they were Latinos from our community.

There are approximately 900 teachers in the Bethlehem Area School District, and they sat it out, not taking sides on the issue in public. Most agreed with me privately, but there were 100 to 150 Latino teachers who did not agree with me, so the teachers union took no position and was not involved in the debate. They were worried about membership loss, and to this day, that really bothers me. Teachers need to stand up, step up, be accountable, and fight for what they believe in. The bilingual program was eliminated and replaced with an English Acquisition Program. Its goal was "to have all Limited English-Proficient (LEP) students become fluent in English in the shortest amount of time, so they may experience maximum success in school." This is what the program is supposed to do. Period! We no longer work on maintaining culture. We do not teach self-esteem. We have stopped segregating Latino students into enclaves within our school district, and these students are integrated with their English-speaking classmates in the mainstream classrooms of all our schools.

I am happy to report that the English Acquisition Program has been successful and has proven to be a much better approach than our old bilingual program. LEP students are being exited at a faster rate than in the old program. Data are available upon request. However, there are three additional stumbling blocks negatively affecting our Latino students in the Bethlehem Area School District. These blocks are societal rather than educational issues: poverty, dysfunctional families, and mobility. Poverty and dysfunctionality within families cross ethnic lines and have the same negative effects on young people regardless of racial or ethnic background. But the one unique problem associated with Latinos is mobility. They move in and out of our district at a rapid pace. We cannot get our arms around them long enough to help them. If, as a society, we could solve those three serious problems, the children coming from impoverished homes with no specific stability in their lives would finally get the true benefits that can be derived from an education. Due to our program improvement, we are making progress, but we still have a long way to go because of the remaining societal issues that have yet to be solved by anyone in this country.

There is yet another factor contributing to the problem in Bethlehem, a cultural barrier to academic achievement, and I suspect it may be affecting the ultimate success of Latino students across the country. There is a code among young, especially male, Latinos that if they do well in school they are acting like the "white kids." Therefore, unfortunately, within the teenage subculture there is an incentive not to do well because they want to maintain their own identity. Enough Latino students and parents have told me this that I believe it to be an issue. In fact, Latino students who have gotten into trouble in our school district, as well as those who have gone on to major colleges and universities, have confirmed this. A lot of peer pressure is put on young Latinos "not to do what the white kids do." Truly, this fact baffles and worries me, and we in Bethlehem have yet to figure out what to do about it.

Throughout this country, the bilingual vs. English acquisition debate has become highly politicized. Judges and legislators are telling us what and how to teach in our classrooms. Even the research is highly questionable. The National Association for Bilingual Education (NABE) passed a resolution a few years back censuring me because we had the courage to start an English Acquisition Program in Bethlehem.

I understand that bilingual education is a battleground, unfortunately, in American ethnic politics. But, we owe all our children the finest education possible, an education that will ensure that this generation receives all the advantages available in this great country. Without a good command of the English language as soon as possible, this dream will never be fulfilled.

—

(Editor's note: The complete text of "Four-Year Longitudinal Report for the English Acquisition Program in the Bethlehem, Pennsylvania, Area School District," by Ann Goldberg, was published in the Fall 1998 issue of *READ Perspectives*, Vol. V-2. The Executive Summary of the article is reprinted at the end of the conference papers, on page 128, as Appendix 4.)

RESTRUCTURING SCHOOLS TO INCORPORATE LINGUISTICALLY DIVERSE POPULATIONS

Rosalie Porter: The last speaker on our panel, Professor Maria Brisk, hardly needs an introduction. She is certainly the best-known professor of bilingual education in Massachusetts, and she enjoys a national reputation as well.

María Estela Brisk: According to the 1990 census, there are 6.3 million school age children in the United States who speak a language other than English at home (Waggoner, 1993). These students come to school with some or no knowledge of English. Schools handle them by the "sink-or-swim" method or by providing special programs. In the "sink-or-swim" method, students are placed at their appropriate grade level and left to their own devices. The special programs include English as a Second Language (ESL) and bilingual education. In the ESL programs students receive intensive training in the English language as part of the school day. Bilingual education involves the use of English and the students' native language for instruction. Most bilingual education programs are transitional in nature. In these programs students are mainstreamed into English-speaking classes when they have acquired mastery in English. While in the program, students' native language and culture are included in the curriculum, but there is intense pressure to learn English. Once they leave the bilingual program, their language and culture are ignored. Some schools have bilingual programs for English-speaking students as well as students who speak another language. These programs use two languages for instruction throughout schooling. They have as a goal bilingualism for all (Lindholm, 1990).

There is much debate as to which model works best. In practice, models matter less than the individual features of particular programs. A number of conditions distinguish successful educational programs for bilingual learners (see Brisk, 1998, for a full treatment). One important characteristic is the integration of the bilingual program into the whole school without sacrificing the goals or structure of the program. Successful bilingual programs are featured in the school's educational agenda as an integral ingredient in the school's mission (Carter & Chatfield, 1986). While bilingual staff should understand the academic goals of the schools and incorporate them into their curricula regardless of the language of instruction, administration and other staff should recognize the bilingual program's goals and support its approach to education. The bilingual program curriculum must be planned together with the whole school's curriculum, bilingual program staff must be considered active members of the school faculty, and bilingual students should be the responsibility of all the staff. When a middle school with bilingual students restructured to form interdisciplinary clusters, the school included the bilingual students in its plan. The school staffed one of the clusters with bilingual staff in the various disciplines as well as including bilingual faculty members in each of the other clusters. In this way, the needs of bilingual students are considered in all school clusters, while the students in the transitional program are fully served by the bilingual cluster.

Integration of the bilingual program is not complete without bringing the students together in academic and social contexts. Bilingual schools and two-way bilingual programs integrate students by design because such programs include English speakers as well as speakers of other languages. Both groups learn both languages and cultures. Schools with bilingual and mainstream programs serving separate populations can also integrate students without sacrificing the bilingual nature of the education.

Desirable educational outcomes for bilingual students include language and literacy development, academic achievement, and sociocultural integration (Brisk, 1998). Bringing students together helps accomplish linguistic and academic goals, as well as achieving socio-cultural integration. Feeling unthreatened by speakers of other languages is an essential educational goal for both bilingual and English-speaking students. Bilingual students must learn to function not only in their ethnic community but also in the larger English-speaking society. In turn, English-speaking students need to learn to feel comfortable around peers of other cultures who use a language they do not understand, and who are in the process of learning English but still cannot express themselves clearly. Language tolerance lays an important foundation for acquisition of a second language, a goal required by most educational reform movements.

Integration can be accomplished in a variety of ways (Brisk, 1991a, 1991b; De Jong, 1996, 1997). The purpose of this article is to describe a bilingual/bicultural approach used to integrate students where both languages and cultures have equal status. In such programs bilingual and mainstream students and faculty work together as equals. The school leadership incorporates the goals of integration into the whole school goals and structure in order to facilitate implementation.

BILINGUAL INTEGRATED EDUCATION

Bilingual integrated education was tested in a school district with a large number of students of diverse linguistic backgrounds, most of whom are Spanish speakers. This school system teaches in English to native speakers of English as well as to bilingual students with adequate English fluency. The system also provides Transitional Bilingual Education (TBE) for students who are at the initial stages of learning English. Content area subjects as well as literacy are offered in the native language while the students learn English. Within three years, most of the students are transferred to mainstream classes. Except for individual teachers' efforts, students in the TBE program have very little contact with mainstream students. The project was carried out by integrating existing classrooms without need for special funding. Selected bilingual and mainstream classes formed clusters. School principals facilitated the process, and teachers fully participated in shaping the implementation of the project. The remainder of this article describes the structure of clusters, the essential elements required for implementation, and the effects of the approach.

STRUCTURE OF CLUSTERS

Clusters were either partially or fully integrated. Partial integration was characterized by careful coordination of the teachers in the cluster around a theme or discipline, with weekly contact among the students in the cluster. Full integration implied coordination in all disciplines with daily contact among students in the cluster. First- and second-grade teachers formed partially integrated clusters, while the fifth and seventh grades were fully integrated. Although full integration is the ideal, partial integration allowed younger bilingual students to have more time for literacy and content area instruction in the native language. In the long run, emphasis on instruction in the native language in the early grades has positive effects in academic performance in the second language (Campos & Keatinge, 1988; Ramirez, 1992).

First- and second-grade clusters consisted of one bilingual and one mainstream teacher and their students. Working around a theme or discipline, the two teachers planned activities together to be carried out in their respective classes. As usual, the bilingual teacher taught most of the lesson in Spanish while the mainstream teacher instructed in English. Once a week the whole cluster worked together on an activity related to the weekly theme. Some clusters assembled in one room with all the students and the two teachers; others divided the students so that each teacher worked in her own classroom with a mixed group of students. When the classes were mixed, the students were free to use either language. The bilingual teacher instructed in Spanish and English while the mainstream teacher instructed in English. Each student had a partner from the other class. These pairs worked in groups of four or eight students. For example, first-grade students from each classroom paired up for a math game related to that week's lesson. The bilingual and mainstream teacher took turns to explain the task in Spanish and English. The bilingual teacher taught the basic vocabulary to the whole class in both languages. As the pairs began the game, the teachers walked around answering questions and observing the work.

Fifth- and seventh-grade level clusters were fully integrated, but they organized themselves in different ways. Fifth-grade teachers taught all subject matters. The bilingual teacher taught in Spanish only when she had all Spanish-speaking students, and in Spanish and English when she had a mixed group. The mainstream teachers taught in English, using the assistance of the more fluent bilingual students for clarification. Students were assigned to classes depending on their language proficiency and needs. Criteria for assignment included language ability, math skill level, need to experience content fully in native language, and need to experience content in second language. Teachers constantly conferred about particular students and made readjustments in the assignments when needed.

Each of three seventh-grade teachers taught math and one other discipline. For math instruction, students were divided into three groups by ability, regardless of language proficiency. Each teacher worked with one group. For the other disciplines, students were assigned to one of three groups. One group was mostly recent arrivals who could best communicate in Spanish. The other two groups were mixed. Thus, the bilingual science teacher taught science in Spanish to the first group but bilingually to the other two groups. The reading and language arts teacher taught Spanish literature and ESL to the first group and English literature to the other two groups. The social studies teacher, who was English-speaking, taught in English but introduced the vocabulary bilingually and provided readings in Spanish. The bilingual teacher aide worked with her during social studies. In the fifth- and seventh-grade clusters, students formed integrated groups for specialists such as music, computer, and art. Each cluster participated together in field trips, playground activities, lunch, holiday celebrations, and after-school sports.

ESSENTIAL CHARACTERISTICS

Certain elements were identified as essential to accomplish the goals of this approach. These include equality of status for all members in the cluster, clear understanding of the program, freedom of language use, classroom methodologies that encourage student interaction and initiative, a coordinated curriculum, and program flexibility in order to meet individual students' needs.

All students and teachers in each cluster had equal status. Teachers were responsible for all students. In turn, students felt equally comfortable relating to all teachers. Each teacher preserved her own class-room, but all students and teachers in the cluster felt free to go in and out of all the classrooms. The classrooms were located close to one another to facilitate the flow of students. Changing classes did not take longer than three to five minutes. For example, one of the bilin-gual first-grade teachers had brought a cocoon so that the students could observe a live caterpillar in the process of metamorphosis to a butterfly. All first-graders in that cluster came to the teacher's room first thing in the morning to check on the cocoon and note any changes in their science notebook. Mainstream students would then go on to their own room to start the morning session.

The concept of the program was introduced to students and parents at the beginning of the year. Special activities helped the initial encoun-ter among students. A positive first experience among students who are not used to working together is essential in establishing a positive relationship among the members of the cluster. For example, one first-grade cluster gave half of a picture to each student in the bilingual class and the other half to each student in the mainstream class. The two students whose halves matched worked as partners for the rest of the period. In looking for the other half of the puzzle, students had to inter-act with one another, thus quickly breaking barriers between the groups. It is also important to reassure parents that their children will be learning in this new social structure. For example, the parents of the fifth- grade cluster attended an abbreviated version of a day in school. One evening, teachers staged ten-minute renditions of their classes. Parents followed their own child from class to class to get the flavor of the program.

Regardless of the language of instruction, the language of the stu-dents was accepted at all times. In the case of this school district, it meant more than Spanish and English; Khmer, Chinese, Czech, and many other languages were represented. All languages were consid-ered valid for solving problems, asking for clarification, reading, and writing. When there was limited proficiency of the language either on the part of the teacher or the student, various strategies were used to facilitate comprehension, such as translation by bilingual individu-als, or use of pictures, gestures, and hands-on activities. In this con-text students understood that communication difficulties were not evidence of language problems, but rather of a problematic situation which required creative solutions.

The methodologies used were appropriate for students with a variety of language levels, both in their native and second languages. Teachers usually introduced the daily lesson to the whole class. The bilingual teachers alternated the languages, while the English-speaking teachers would ask a bilingual student, student-teacher or teacher-aide to translate. Following the introduction, students worked on specific tasks in groups. The teacher and any other adult in the class walked around the classroom answering questions, clarifying tasks, and checking comprehension. Group work is an essential form of organization for heterogeneous classrooms (DeVillar & Faltis, 1991). Because of the variety of literacy and math ability levels, cross-age projects were organized to reinforce language and math skills. Older students acted as expert tutors rather than learners in need of remediation. While being trained as tutors for the younger students, the older students' literacy and math skills were reinforced. Students in the fifth- and seventh-grade clusters taught reading, writing, and math in either English or Spanish to kindergarten, first- or second-graders in either bilingual or mainstream classes.

Together, teachers planned a coordinated curriculum reinforcing the connections among the classrooms. Thematic units, coordination of content across disciplines, and content-area subjects supporting class projects were among the strategies used. For example, two first grade teachers developed monthly units involving all disciplines around a particular theme. This theme was carried out when they were with their own students as well as when they were in integrated groups. The teachers shared materials and ideas.

Teachers also met to decide on each student's plan of study based on language ability and needs. For example, when Carlos, a recent arrival from El Salvador, entered fifth grade the teachers decided that he would take reading, language arts, and social studies in Spanish; math and ESL in a bilingual class; and some science units bilingually and some in English. Thus he was receiving most of the instruction in the language he understood best but was being exposed to English through language teaching as well as through a content area. On the other hand Jennifer, an English-speaking student, took all her classes with English-speaking teachers except for math. Taking math with the bilingual teacher met Jennifer's needs to take high-level math and to experience Spanish in an academic context. During their weekly meetings, the teachers discussed their students and made adjustments in their schedule when necessary.

EFFECTS OF THE BILINGUAL INTEGRATED APPROACH

The intended academic and social goals were accomplished. In addition, this approach had a surprising effect on the value placed on bilingualism. The following academic goals were met:

> **Goal 1: To give all students access to a complete and comprehensible academic curriculum.**

In most cases, bilingual students received instruction in the language they could understand best, and the teachers used instructional strategies that facilitated comprehension when the instruction was in the students' weaker language. Problems occurred when a particular discipline was taught by a monolingual English-speaking teacher, as was the case in seventh-grade social studies. All students had to take social studies in English when a bilingual teacher was not available. The fifth-grade cluster avoided this problem because all teachers taught all disciplines, so recent arrivals were placed mostly in bilingual classes.

> **Goal 2: To provide a functional and friendly setting to learn English as a Second Language.**

To varying degrees, all students found themselves in a class where a discipline was taught in English. The atmosphere in this class, however, recognized that the student had intellectual abilities in another language—all that had to be solved was a communication problem. Bilingual students developed their second language in a functional and unthreatening setting, two important conditions for second language learning (Spolsky, 1989).

"Antes no me gustaba oir que habian maestras que solo hablaban inglés, pero ahora si me gusta porque sé que entre más inglés oiga, más inglés voy a aprender. Al principio creía que iba a costar aprender inglés, pero gracias a Dios no me está costando." (Student in bilingual program)

[Before I did not like to listen to teachers who only spoke English, but now I like it because the more English I hear the more English I'll learn. At first I thought it would be too hard, but thank goodness, it is not hard.]

In this project, great emphasis was put on social integration. The following social goals were met:

Goal 1: To eliminate the isolation of bilingual programs.

Students and teachers considered themselves part of a group where all members had equal status regardless of their ability in English. There were no distinctions between students officially enrolled in the bilingual program and mainstream students, thus the stigma of remediation was eliminated. One of the bilingual students specifically mentioned being pleased that he was finally in "the regular school." Therefore he no longer felt isolated in a special program although he was indeed officially in the bilingual program. The lines between bilingual and mainstream programs became invisible to students. To accommodate students' needs and bilingual programs' rules, teachers gave students their assignments without labeling and separating them as bilingual or mainstream students. In almost every cluster, however, there were one or two students from either the bilingual or mainstream classes who took a long time to feel comfortable with integration. This problem arises because students view the bilingual program as a remedial program; consequently, they want to disassociate themselves from it.

"When I first came here, I didn't really want to stay in this home room [integrated]. 'Cause ... I didn't want to be in a Spanish and English class. But now ... one of the students is already my best friend, and I like Miss M., my math teacher [English speaker]... And now I think is [sic] great that I'm in this program." (Mainstreamed Spanish-speaking student, four months after the program started)

Goal 2: To integrate students in an academic setting.

Often schools organize multicultural festivals as a way to recognize the presence of different cultural groups. These activities provide only a glimpse of people's culture and preserve the quaint character of it. By bringing together students in an academic setting, the bilingual integrated program gave English-speaking students the opportunity to encounter Spanish in relation to academic disciplines. This experience helped them change their perspective toward the Spanish culture beyond food and dance. For example, James, a monolingual, English-speaking student, expressed it in this manner: "I like it [the integrated program] because I can learn some words of Spanish for the future ... if I became a teacher I can speak Spanish in the classroom."

Goal 3: To have bilingual students participate in classes taught by mainstream teachers as insiders not outsiders.

Unlike the typical fear experienced by bilingual students in mainstream classrooms (Brisk, 1991c, 1994), students in this program felt welcomed by English-speaking teachers and students. As a result these students learned to deal without fear with English-speaking people and dared to use their incipient English.

"Yo me siento bien al estar cambiando con los niños Americanos que no saben hablar español y la maestra tampoco sabe hablarlo. Asi yo me tengo que esforzarme en el inglés para poder entender y cada día aprendo cosas nuevas y tengo más amigos." (Bilingual student)

[I feel good relating to American kids who do not speak Spanish and the teacher doesn't know it either. This way I have to make an effort in English to try to understand. Every day I learn new things and have more friends.]

Commins (1989) found that even when Spanish-speaking children wanted to speak English, they rarely interacted with English-speaking peers. This, she speculates, may have "hindered the students' development of full proficiency in English" (p. 36).

Goal 4: To allow participation in the bilingual program to students who have been "officially" mainstreamed.

In the typical transitional model, once students are mainstreamed they usually no longer have contact with the bilingual program. This is particularly true with elementary school students (Section III, MacDonald et al., 1982). Moreover, students are usually mainstreamed long before they have native-like mastery of academic English. Collier

(1989) found that students take longer than three years—the usual stay in the TBE program—to function in academic English at the level of native speakers. Therefore, bilingual students can benefit from access to a bilingual teacher long after they have been officially mainstreamed. For example, two mainstreamed Puerto Rican fifth-graders were having great difficulty writing in English. The teachers decided that intensive writing in Spanish would establish a basis for moving on to writing in English. The two students then were placed in language arts with the bilingual teacher. Simultaneously, they were taking all other courses in English. Another unforeseen benefit for mainstreamed bilingual students was the ability to keep friends. As one Spanish-speaking mainstreamed student mentioned, "I like going to Mrs. H's [bilingual teacher's] class because all the kids there were in fourth grade with me." With this approach students can be officially mainstreamed without being separated from their friends who are still "officially" in the bilingual program.

Goal 5: To teach all students and teachers that thinking and learning can happen in languages other than English.

Although it took some adjustment on the part of teachers and English-speaking students, Spanish was accepted as a viable means for learning. English-speaking teachers made an effort to find readings and texts in Spanish for students who wanted to use them. Group discussions, writings, and reports were also accepted in Spanish. This change in attitude toward use of Spanish was followed by acceptance of other languages. For example, shortly after Alex arrived from Czechoslovakia, the teacher gave a science test. Students had to write the names of the bones in a picture of the skeleton. Alex wrote his in Czech and got full credit for his work. The teacher and some of his classmates worked with him in teaching him the English names. This same teacher the previous year did not allow bilingual students in her class to use a language other than English.

Goal 6: To create an environment where English-speaking students and teachers learn to feel comfortable around speakers of other languages and students of different cultures.

Initially, some English-speaking students—and even some mainstreamed Spanish-speaking students—were uncomfortable hearing Spanish in the mainstream classes where traditionally it had been forbidden. Eventually, most students became used to it and many of the English speakers started to learn some Spanish naturally. For example, when a group of English-speaking seventh-graders complained early in the year that two boys "were speaking too much Spanish," the Spanish-speaking boys reacted by offering Spanish lessons during their morning break. The English speakers readily submitted and soon began showing off their Spanish with the bilingual teachers.

Students learned to treat one another as equals. As one of the teachers pointed out, the problems that arose were due to the fact that these students were children rather than to any cultural prejudices. English-speaking students for the first time had the experience of working with bilingual teachers. The students learned to respect adults of a different ethnic background and at the same time had good role models of bilingualism in the bilingual teachers whose native language was English.

The teachers in turn developed respect for one another. Mainstream and bilingual teachers learned to trust that they could teach one another's students. Meeting weekly, sharing observations and concerns, and focusing on their strengths paved the way for mutual trust among teachers. They took advantage of one another's strengths to organize the curriculum and develop activities.

Additional Effects
In addition to accomplishing the initial goals of the program, other unplanned effects were observed. Among them were the value placed on bilingualism, development of positive attitudes toward languages, a clear sense of identity for bilingual students, and ties with parents of mainstream bilingual students. A high level of bilingualism became a great asset. The greatest effect was on those bilingual students with advanced proficiency in English. Due to their English proficiency, these students were neglecting their Spanish and many did not even want to admit they knew it. In the integrated settings, however, these bilingual students became extremely important to facilitate communication between newly arrived Spanish speakers and monolingual English-speaking teachers and students.

"I help Mrs. K. and Mrs. P. [English-speaking teachers]. When kids don't understand in English, I explain in Spanish.... My mother and father will be proud of me because this year I will learn a lot. This is AWESOME!" (Mainstreamed Spanish-speaking student)

Acceptance of one's native language by English speakers can be a motivator for learning English (Schumann, 1978). Newly arrived bilingual students showed a desire to learn English in order to communicate with their new friends without feeling that they had to neglect their own language. Thus, bilingual students accepted themselves and were accepted by others as bilingual/bicultural individuals. Learning English did not mean they had to ignore their identity as bilingual individuals. Bilingual students function much better in school when they fully accept both languages (Gardner & Lambert, 1972; Bhatnagar, 1980).

Usually, parents of bilingual children who have been mainstreamed lose contact with their children's school because they do not dare communicate with English-speaking teachers. In this integrated setting all teachers met with all parents, thus the bilingual teacher could help with translation when a bilingual parent came to school. Even in the case of a Czech parent, the bilingual Spanish-speaking teacher facilitated the communication because of her experience dealing with parents of different cultures and limited English proficiency.

CONCLUSION

In the United States during this past century, we have gone through a process of first neglecting the educational needs of linguistically diverse populations and then to developing mostly transitional bilingual education programs that are compensatory in nature and that mostly segregate students from the rest of the school children. The dilemma of populations with needs that schools have not traditionally addressed is how to meet these needs while avoiding isolation and detrimental labels (Minow, 1990). The purpose of this article is to show how, through a bilingual integrated approach, one can change the remedial and segregated nature of education for linguistically diverse students without eliminating instruction in these students' native languages. Bilingual and mainstream labels disappear, while teachers focus on individual needs.

In a world that is being characterized by increasing displacement of populations we need to rethink our strategies of absorbing immigrants and the role education plays in the process. Learning from the experience in the United States, other countries in the process of addressing the needs of linguistically diverse populations should ensure the integration of these populations within the school community. The whole school should embrace these students to give them an appropriate education. In turn, populations of the host country need to be educated to interact with immigrants and help them in their adjustment to the new society by accepting their language and culture.

Taylor (1987), based on Berry's work, proposes four orientations that people can adopt to cope with diversity: assimilation, separation, deculturation, and integration. Assimilation views diversity as harmful; separation supports maintenance of native languages and cultures, but promotes separation from the national culture; deculturation is the result of lack of identity with either group; and integration views the maintenance of the languages and cultures of diverse populations as a way to enhance the opportunities for intergroup cooperation. The educational solution proposed in this article subscribes to the integration ideology in which allowing groups to retain their heritage and identity is considered the best route to incorporation in a new society.

REFERENCES

Bhatnagar, J.K. (1980). Linguistic behavior and adjustment of immigrant children in French and English schools in Montreal. *International Review of Applied Psychology, 2,* pp. 141–158.

Brisk, M.E. (1991a). Toward multilingual and multicultural mainstream education. *Journal of Education,* 173, No. 2, pp.114–129.

Brisk, M.E. (1991b). Cross cultural barriers, a model for schooling bilingual and english-speaking students in harmony. *Equity and Choice,* 7, No. 2, pp. 18–24.

Brisk, M.E. (1991c). *The many voices of bilingual students in Massachusetts.* Quincy, MA: Bureau of Equity and Language Services, Massachusetts Department of Education.

Brisk, M.E. (1994). *Portraits of success: Resources supporting bilingual learners.* Boston, MA: National Association for Bilingual Education.

Brisk, M. E. (1998). *Bilingual education: From compensatory to quality schooling.* Mahwah, NJ.

Campos, S.J. & Keatinge, R.H. (1988). The Carpintería language minority student experience. In T. Skutnabb-Kangas and Jim Cummins (Eds.), *Minority education: From shame to struggle* (pp. 299–307). Clevedon, England: Multilingual Matters.

Carter, T. & Chatfield, M. (1986). Effective schools for language minority students. *American Journal of Education, 97,* 200–233.

Collier, V. P. (1989). How long? A synthesis of research on academic achievement in a second language. *TESOL Quarterly,* 23, pp. 509–531.

Commins, N.L. (1989). Language and affect: Bilingual students at home and at school. *Language Arts,* 66, pp. 29–41.

Cummins, J. (1984). *Bilingualism and special education: Issues in assessment and pedagogy.* Clevedon, England: Multilingual Matters.

De Jong, E. (1996). Integrating language minority education in elementary schools. Unpublished doctoral dissertation, Boston University.

De Jong, E. (1997). School policy and learning in bilingual contexts. In J.N. Jorgensen & A. Holment (Eds.), *The development of successive bilingualsim in school-age children.* Copenhagen: Royal Danish School of Educational Studies.

DeVillar, R.A. & Faltis, C.J. (1991). *Computers and cultural diversity: Restructuring for school success.* Albany, NY: State University of New York Press.

Gardner, R.C. & Lambert. (1972). *Attitudes and motivation in second language learning.* Rowley, MA: Newbury House Publishers.

Lindholm, K. (1990). Bilingual immersion education. Criteria for program development. In Padilla, A.M., Fairchild, H.H. & Valadez, C. (Eds.), *Bilingual education: Issues and strategies,* pp. 91–105. Newbury Park, CA: Sage Publications.

MacDonald, B., Aldeman, C., Kushner, S., & Walker, R. (1982). *Bread and dreams: A case study of bilingual schooling in the U.S.A.* Norwich, UK: Centre for Applied Research in Education, University of East Anglia.

Minow, Martha. (1990). *Making all the difference: Inclusion, exclusion, and American law.* Ithaca, NY: Cornell University Press.

Ramirez, J.D. (1992). Executive Summary. *Bilingual Research Journal,* 16, 1–62.

Schumann, J. (1978). *The pidginization process: A model for second language acquisition*. Rowley, MA: Newbury House.

Spolsky, B. (1989). *Conditions for second language learning*. Oxford: Oxford University Press.

Taylor, Donald M. (1987). Social psychological barriers to effective childhood bilingualism. In P. Hornel, M. Palij, & D. Aaronson (Eds.), *Childhood bilingualism: Aspects of linguistic, cognitive and social development* (pp. 183–195). Hillsdale, NJ: Lawrence Erlbaum Associates.

Waggoner, D. (1993). The growth of multilingualism and the need for bilingual education: What do we know so far? *Bilingual Research Journal, 17*, 1/2, pp. 1–12.

KEYNOTE SPEAKER RICHARD M. ESTRADA

Rosalie Porter: Our guest speaker, Richard M. Estrada, came from Dallas today to give us his thoughts on bilingual education. I have been acquainted with Richard since 1990 when he called me to say some very kind things about my first book. We renewed our acquaintance recently in Dallas, just a few weeks ago, when I was speaking to the Education Writers Association and Richard was very much a part of the discussion.

Our guest speaker, Mr. Estrada, has been associate editor of the editorial page for the *Dallas Morning News* since 1992. He is also a syndicated columnist for the *Washington Post* Writers Group. A native of New Mexico, Mr. Estrada is fluent in English and Spanish. He has lived in various cities in the United States, as well as in the Panama Canal Zone.

In July 1998, the National Alliance for the Mentally Ill bestowed on Mr. Estrada its 1998 award for editorial writing on mental health issues. Since September 1998, Richard has been writing frequent editorials and columns on the issue of bilingual education in California and Texas.

From 1992 until the end of 1997, Mr. Estrada served on the prestigious, congressionally-appointed U.S. Commission on Immigration Reform that was headed by the late Barbara Jordan, a U.S. House representative from Texas. In the course of his work on the Commission, Richard visited many cities in the United States to hold hearings on the needs of immigrant students and their schooling. We welcome Richard Estrada.

Richard Estrada: Thank you very much for having me here today. If I may, I'd like to concentrate here on the question of bilingual education in Texas, and give you my perspective on this issue, as someone from the Southwest. It is a perspective that has developed and undergone something of a metamorphosis over the last few decades.

Before I do that, however, perhaps I should tell you something about myself. I do not consider myself to be typical of the student population or those who were once students in the Mexican-American school districts of the Southwest, and I don't want to give that impression.

What was different about my situation is that my father, whose parents were impoverished immigrants from Mexico, was a military officer; and as a result, I grew up in various cities around the United States, including cities in the Southwest. El Paso, for example, I consider to be my stomping ground.

I think this is very important because if there is one thing I believe in very deeply, it is that the role models you have closest to you in your family have an enormous impact on how things turn out. My father made it very clear to me, from my earliest days, that I was to learn English as well as I could; that was to be the most important issue for me. At the same time, he insisted that I learn Spanish. But he taught me Spanish, and he taught me not only through our conversations, but also in taking me across the river to see Chihuahua, Chihuahua City, Panama City. Eventually as a journalist, I started going on my own to places like Mexico City, the Dominican Republic, Cuba, and to other places in Latin America.

That kind of experience growing up is not typical of Mexican-American students and Mexican immigrant students in the Southwest.

As I look back at what has happened in the bilingual education debate over the past several years, one thing strikes me, and I think that it bears noting and reflecting on by everyone. That is, when Senator Ralph Yarborough, the Texas Democrat who pushed through bilingual education back in the late 1960s, was addressing this issue, clearly one of the things that was most on his mind was the issue of Mexican-American poverty and Mexican-American dropout rates in Texas. At that time, the question of Chicano rural poverty also was uppermost in the minds of many people.

Today, the issue is a very different one. Increasingly, for all the talk about the *colonias* along the border, in isolated regions, the issue is increasingly one of urban poverty among Hispanic-origin kids, not only from Mexico or of Mexican origin, but also from Central America and elsewhere.

What we see here—in Houston, in Dallas, in San Antonio, in particular—is an enormous increase in the numbers, which is projected to increase even more in the next century.

Why do I make this point? Well, for one thing, the question of addressing the educational needs of Mexican-origin students who may not have had a good command of English back in the 1960s is very different when you look at the situation today. If you look at immigration and language research over the years, it is often noted that the question of large linguistic enclaves present a unique challenge.

If you look at East Los Angeles today, one thing that has to be noted right away is that a young person who goes to school and learns some English is going to have a very difficult time getting that English reinforced out on the street or on his trip to the grocery store or in conversations with his parents. The absolute concentration of non-English speakers oftentimes serves to inhibit the learning of English in these particular areas.

I think in places like Dallas, San Antonio, and Houston, we are very rapidly beginning to see this, and so the challenge is of a different magnitude, perhaps, than what we've had in the past. It also opens to question whether the kinds of approaches we saw back in the early years of bilingual education are still relevant to the current problems that we're facing.

To give you an idea of what we are facing in Texas today, I brought along a few statistics that might help you compare to the situations that you're most familiar with. There were about 514,139 limited-English students enrolled in Texas public schools in 1996–97. This number represented about 13 percent of the total student body.

Between 1992–93 and 1996–97, the Limited-English Proficient population increased by 29 percent, compared to an 8 percent increase in the total student population over the same period.

In Texas, about 91 percent of Limited-English Proficient students speak Spanish. In the Dallas Independent school district, about 97 percent of the children who are in the bilingual education programs speak Spanish.

So those statistics really must be kept in mind because we're talking about a particular group of kids, and the variations in responses to bilingual education programs that you see among different ethnic groups is not the same in Texas as it might be in, for example, California or elsewhere in the country.

Students with limited English proficiency (LEP) are less likely to be receiving special education services, but 87 percent are receiving bilingual education or ESL services. This is a point that I think is particularly relevant to our discussion today. In 1996–97, more than 87 percent of Limited-English Proficient students were economically disadvantaged compared to 48 percent of non-LEP students.

As I ponder this issue and write editorials about it, it seems to me that much of the bilingual education debate has been over pedagogical themes considered in a vacuum. I'm not saying that you do not have to have a comparison among different pedagogical approaches, but I would say that these enormous shifts in population, the development, the growth of poverty, especially in the urban areas of cities in Texas and elsewhere in the country, absolutely have to be considered.

This has to be looked at from a longitudinal perspective, and the failure to do so, I think, is going to put us at a disadvantage in identifying those particular approaches that tend to help kids make the transition from Spanish to English. I do not mean by this that these kids can't simultaneously develop a greater expertise in Spanish, if they so desire.

I think this also calls for a greater discussion, a shift in the focus of the discussion, in which we are very honest with one another about the fact that this is not just about pedagogical approaches; it is also about the changes that we're witnessing in society.

One of the biggest changes, of course, has to do with immigration. My service on the U.S. Commission on Immigration Reform has already been mentioned. I will also note that the majority of the members were appointed by the congressional leadership, both Republican and Democrat, in the Senate and in the House, and the chair was appointed by the president.

What we have to do in looking at the bilingual education issue is to be very honest concerning what the political debate is really about in today's terms. In my view, the bilingual education debate is too often about things other than the education of Limited-English Proficient students, and I think we have to be very honest in acknowledging that. At certain times, it can be an immigration debate; at other times, it can be a debate over how best to handle the education of all public school students. Increasingly, I fear the issue of school choice is motivating a number of people who wish to do away with any special programs for particular groups.

Now, I don't want to take that too far, because that would imply that I somehow am against any kind of reforms. I most certainly am not, and as a matter of fact, I'm here exclusively today as an advocate for reforming bilingual education.

In a place like Dallas, Texas, the question of being honest about the bilingual education debate is very, very important because of the rapidity with which we are witnessing the growth in the numbers of these students. I called up the Dallas Independent School District this morning to get the latest statistics, and of a total district enrollment of 160,000 kids, we now have 45,782 children in bilingual and ESL programs.

Within the next five years, fully one-half of all students in the Dallas Independent School District are projected to need some form of special language instruction, whether bilingual or ESL. The average annual growth in student enrollment in these programs has been almost 10 percent; last year it was more than 11 percent.

This is not unique to Dallas. Increasingly, it is an indication of what is happening in the larger cities in the rest of the state, and it is an indicator of where the state as a whole is going in the next century. We have come very rapidly to understand that the days of having one dominant ethnic group in Texas are at an end.

This—to return to my theme of what this debate is really about—has a lot of people worried. To some people, the issue is not just immigration, per se; it can also be about race; it can be about affirmative action. All of these things are, to one degree or another, on people's minds when you ask them about their opinions on bilingual education.

Stephen Murdock, who is a demographer at Texas A&M University, has written very extensively about what Texas is going to look like early in the next century, and as he points out, the issue isn't just that Texas is going to become increasingly more Hispanic. The issue isn't just that more and more Texans are going to speak only or mainly Spanish. The issue is that so much of this new constituency in the State of Texas is going to be impoverished, unless there is a massive change in the approach of the state legislature as to how much we fund education in Texas.

In that context, it is unlikely that there will be enough additional resources to meet this enormous growth in demand for expanded educational services for this group. That is problematic, because, to be very explicit, it implies that the traditional Hispanic origin underclass in Texas is going to be even more of an underclass in the future.

To look at the big picture, when we talk about this immigration issue and put it together with the bilingual education issue, one thing that we ought never forget is that we are currently in the first wave of immigration in American history in the post-industrial era. We are in an economy at this moment where it is absolutely essential for young people to gain the linguistic and communication skills that will allow them to even be minimally competitive today.

Again, let us get away strictly from the question of ideology or pedagogy and look at the real world in which this debate is being staged. An inability to look at these larger issues, at the same time we try to get a handle on how best to help these children, is going to result in a situation that will undermine us all, regardless of which constituency, which group, we tend to belong to.

I think Texas is a somewhat extreme example, but keep in mind that we're also talking, obviously, about California. Ron Unz [a Silicon Valley entrepreneur who sponsored Proposition 227 to reform bilingual education] has done an incredible job in attacking some of the shibboleths out there in California, but increasingly I see a lot of conflict in places like Florida, and even though there's a tremendous bilingual education bureaucracy in New York, I think the real-world problems that New York is facing are going to have to be addressed. Things will get more contentious out there, although not to the degree that you'll see in California or Texas or Florida. I also think that Chicago increasingly is going to have enormous problems in this regard.

So once again, I keep hammering home at this message. But I do want you to see it as the central message of what I'm bringing here today. Looking only at the pedagogical issue is not going to be particularly useful.

I, myself, am more persuaded by those bilingual education experts who have begun to change their ideological fixations or their pedagogical fixations and have begun to say it's not so important what we call a particular language program; what's important is what the components are and whether they work, and that's where we have to be headed.

Having said that, the issue, if you do look at the specifics of the problem, increasingly is going to turn to the length or the duration of the programs. I happen to think, to put my cards on the table, that language and cultural maintenance should not be a part of the bilingual education agenda. I simply am opposed to that.

I'm not opposed to children retaining or improving their capacity to speak the language of their parents; to the contrary, I think that is one of the glories of America. But I do think that the expenditure of public resources for that purpose is wrong, and I think it is particularly wrong at a time in our history when ideologically we are headed toward some very great challenges in the area of public education. The movement toward school choice around the country cannot possibly help the children who will be left behind to pursue their learning in the country's public schools.

As a result, I believe that the schools are going to have to demonstrate that they are more efficient, that they can transition these children to English more quickly. Does that mean you should have no bilingual education programs? I think there are many people who believe that immersion from the first day is the way to go. I believe that the immersion project in El Paso from a few years ago has some real possibilities.

But at the same time, all of us know there are political realities that have to be dealt with. All of us know that at the end of the day there are going to have to be some compromises. It's my belief that at the very least there should be an acknowledgment that the bilingual education programs in the elementary schools should not last more than three years; hopefully, not more than two. That's my belief.

I have spoken to many bilingual educators in the Dallas Independent School District who say that in fact that's always been what they have tried to do. They have gotten children who have been non-English speakers and have actually transitioned them out of the bilingual education programs in one or two years. And these bilingual educators have used some of the traditional methods associated with transitional bilingual education. It's just that they have a greater belief in the capacities of these children to learn, and they actually prod them along.

On the question of the specifics of the pedagogical approaches, I'm going to leave that to the experts. I am not an expert in that, and I'm not going to pretend to be one, but I am saying that I have seen enough examples of children, even in pre-kindergarten classes in Dallas who have very rapidly learned a great deal of English.

I'll tell you one other thing. As I've talked to people in Dallas and throughout Texas, there is a second concern, and that is the concern over the reality of an internal system of segregation in these classes. It is true that these children attend the same schools, but when they do not attend the same classes, there is inevitably a feeling among many of these children that they are being set aside, seen as different, but different in the sense of being inferior.

Let me give you an anecdote. A few years ago I was talking to a group of young people at a gang intervention program in East Dallas, which has a great many Hispanics. I was bantering with these kids about the problems they had faced—these were middle school kids—and they were telling me that in fact they had very much resented being put in these programs, because the rest of the school saw them as being retarded.

And yet, it got to the point where their self-esteem had sunk so low that they almost used it as a badge of honor, and they told me that it was not coincidental that the name of their gang—East Side Locos—in fact had the same letters at the beginning of each word as ESL. I was absolutely astounded, and yet the more I talked to other young people in the district, young Hispanics in this situation, the more I saw that there was an intense resentment over being segregated internally in the schools.

Now, I'm not saying that all of that internal segregation is avoidable, but most certainly it is something that we have to recognize; we have to recognize also that many of these children want nothing more than to be a part of the community. They don't have an animus toward the language of their parents, but these kids do understand that if they are to be full and participating members in the society, they must learn English quickly and well.

Again, going back to the pre-kindergarten bilingual education class, there were mothers who came for the day, just to talk to me, who mentioned that their children actually sought out young, non-Hispanic white children with whom to play. Why? Because those kids taught these Hispanic children terms in English that they wanted to know, whether the terms pertained to sports or school, whatever.

Again, the benefits of this kind of integration should not be given short shrift. Whatever you may say about an editorialist from the *Dallas Morning News*, whatever you may say about other Hispanic proponents of integration and assimilation in America, these young children are not traitors to their ethnic group; they are youngsters who only know that they want to be part of the society, they do not want to be made fun of, they do not want to be set aside; these are youngsters who actually like to compete on the same basis as everyone else.

If there is a message that I have for you, that's it right there. This issue ought not to be seen as an issue driven by a desire to minimize the cultural or linguistic origins of any group. Certainly, any educated person who is familiar with the Spanish language, to give one example, knows full well the richness of that literature. It is only the uneducated person who would ever want to denigrate that language, to give just one example in this debate.

But at the same time, I assure you that when you consider the statistics that I've mentioned here about the correlation of poverty and these newcomer groups, learning English is absolutely the most important thing they will do in trying to become a success in this country. True, some day it may be that they can become international bankers who will need multilingual skills, and more power to them. But my argument today is, first things first.

[The presentation continues with questions from the audience.]

Question: ...As an educator, I'm also very happy to say that you are really an advocate—maybe you don't know it, but you're an advocate for two-way bilingual/ bicultural programs rather than the monolingual approach of English-only or total immersion programs. Because you're an integrationist, I wanted to talk about how the role of white Anglo-Saxon students, the dominant culture, and their responsibility in Texas of learning the language and the culture of the other group, and about how ... in that form of equality we can talk about truly multicultural respect, rather than the dominance and subordination ... that is constantly attached to bilingual education programs.

Mr. Estrada: I've thought about that question quite a bit. Let me say this. I started out my speech by saying that perhaps I'm not typical of the Mexican-American students who grew up in the Southwest because of the uniqueness of my family situation. At the same time, I don't want to exaggerate that. I got yelled at for speaking Spanish on the playground—the whole nine yards. I'm not going to take out the violins and cry about it, but there clearly was the subordination issue you talk about.

Having said that, it seems to me that there is a debate or discussion to be had about what is the principal motivator, or the principal issue in the question of that kind of discriminatory treatment, and I think that the options, broadly spelled out, are two. Number one, the idea that there's somehow spontaneous discrimination or racism against Hispanics or other groups; number two, the natural tendency of groups of a higher socioeconomic class origin to denigrate those of a lower socioeconomic class origin.

Sometimes, of course, anybody who's read the history of the antebellum American South will understand that you have a melding of the two, that you can have the development of an ideology of racism in order to prolong and perpetuate this superior/subordinate status.

What I'm arguing is that since we are no longer in a system of either debt peonage or slavery, but in one in which civil rights are a far greater reality than they were in the past, that it is now vitally important for us to focus on those issues that allow people to climb the socioeconomic ladder. I'll go back to what I was saying a little while ago. To my mind, making the rapid transition to English is the *sine qua non* in that particular process.

With specific regard to two-way bilingual education, I have to admit to being somewhat conflicted by this because I am sympathetic to some of what you're saying. But, at the same time, I also have to think about the larger debate going on and about budgetary concerns. One question that I've been asking myself is this: In a situation in which the majoritarian community increasingly buys into a two-way bilingual approach, is it in fact going to result in an expansion in funding, or will it perhaps mean a dilution of funding for the special instructional programs of one kind or another for the Hispanic or other Limited-English Proficient groups? That's a question I ask very honestly. I don't mean to imply that I know the answer. I'm just really big on process. I'm really big on asking questions every step of the way.

Second, from an ideological and a philosophical perspective, it seems to me that requiring or demanding that there be two-way bilingualism is fraught with potential pitfalls. I'm not prepared to say I'm totally against it, but anything that demands that other languages be taught is bothersome to me for ideological reasons.

If we were to say these majoritarian students should be strongly urged, that school districts should do everything possible to promote not only bilingualism, but a polyglot student body, then I'm all for that. But the question of requiring and demanding is somewhat problematic to me.

Question: I would like to know what you mean by English language proficiency. Are you talking about the ability to speak English, or are you talking about students mastering subject-matter content taught in English? That's my first question. Then my second question is, what are the attributes of effective schooling that lead to students' ability to master high-level content taught in a second language? What are the attributes of effective programs that might lead to that in the long term?

Mr. Estrada: On both counts, I'm not going to get into it too deeply because I think, in fact, that those are the kinds of pedagogical questions best left to the experts. I will say generally what my approach is, and my feeling is that the question of having a command of the English language is basically that you can both comprehend easily and at the same time can speak the language well enough to be competitive in functioning in your society. As far as the long-term ability to understand higher-order problems, I'll tell you, I'm not here to address that today.

I am open to anyone who wishes to discuss and inform on that issue, but that simply is not my point; I think that's better left for another forum, [with] people who hold themselves out to be experts on the pedagogy.

Question: But you're not making any comments on appropriate pedagogical strategies or techniques to use to get children confident.

Mr. Estrada: No, not really. I think I limited myself to saying those particular elements of programs that tend to work. I would like to see some empirical evidence about that, [about effective programs] and then I don't care what you call it. Just cobble something together and get it done.

Question: Not that I think any of us can really argue with the logic of what you said—

Mr. Estrada: Then why do you? [Laughter]

Question: [Is this debate about] ... illegal entrance into this country, predominantly in California and Texas ... with the influx of immigrants into the country and the demands, restrictions that were placed on them recently, whether this bilingual thing is really an offshoot of the whole question of illegal entry ... [denying services to] people from the healthcare system, the educational system, and if you did away with these programs, maybe we wouldn't have these people here, that kind of thinking. Could you react to that?

Mr. Estrada: I can only react to it by saying what I said and perhaps elaborating a little on it. My view is that the bilingual education debate is sometimes hijacked by people who wish to talk about these other things for whatever reasons they may have. The motives may not have anything to do with what is best or most effective for the children in question. That's my main point.

The second point I would make, however, is that whether you talk about legal immigration or illegal immigration, I believe that there is afoot in this country a wrongheaded notion that policy before the entrance, before the admission of people into this country, doesn't matter. Policy matters very, very much. So what we see in the larger debates over language and immigration is a situation in which people have not wanted to discuss the policy issues extant. And I fear that, as a result, this opens the door for greater demands on curbing the programs that are extended to the newcomers, *ex post*. It is the difference, I would submit, between a discussion over immigration policy and over immigrant policy.

Let me point out that there are many, many polls over the years that have found, repeatedly, that Hispanic Americans are about as concerned over the levels of immigration to America as are most other Americans. At the same time, votes, elections in California and elsewhere, and polls have found that Hispanic Americans are deeply concerned about perceived attacks on immigrant utilization of social service benefits.

So, what you have here is the Hispanic element in the country, in my view, being absolutely logical in drawing the distinction between immigration policy and immigrant policy. And, if I may go one step further, whether in California or in Washington, I think the Republican Party has done itself a great disservice in refusing to address immigration policy but in being very quick to address immigrant policy, which has budgetary consequences.

PANEL III - EDUCATION REFORM IN MASSACHUSETTS

Moderator, Mr. James Peyser, Pioneer Institute

James Peyser: This panel is about education policy, and particularly about education reform in Massachusetts. It is about the relationship between the present status of bilingual education and its evolving nature, and about how changes will affect the limited-English students and the methods for teaching them.

The first panelist is Dr. Charles Glenn, author of *The Myth of the Common School*, which I'm sure many of you have read, and if you haven't, I recommend it to you. I consider it to be my own personal historical bible about public education in this country. He is also the author of *Educating Immigrant Children: Schools and Language Minorities in Twelve Nations*, which provides an interesting and enlightening compendium of analyses of different national approaches to this particular issue.

Next is Representative Harold Lane from Holden, chairman of the Joint Committee on Education, Arts and Humanities in the Massachusetts Legislature. Typically, people have an impression that as legislators rise in the heirarchy, they are given increasing amounts of responsibility over subjects with which they have less and less knowledge. In this case, the situation is reversed. The chairman has had a long career as teacher and administrator in Massachusetts public schools, and he brings these years of experience to bear in his role as education chairman. We're lucky to have him in that role.

After him is Eugene Creedon, superintendent of the Quincy, Massachusetts, Public Schools since 1992. Interestingly, he has spent his entire professional career in the Quincy school system and, in fact, attended the Quincy schools. He's a man with deep knowledge of public education, and certainly about the situation in Quincy schools and about specific conditions in that community.

Then, finally, Douglas Sears, superintendent of the Chelsea, Massachusetts, Public Schools. As you may know, the Chelsea school system has been operating under an agreement with Boston University; and prior to becoming superintendent, Sears was a member of the Chelsea/Boston University Oversight Team. Before his work at Boston University, he served in the U.S. Foreign Service.

With that, let us begin with Charlie Glenn and his ideas on bilingual education reform in Massachusetts.

A Bilingual Supporter Calls for Reform

Charles Glenn: More than ten years ago, I spoke at a meeting of MABE, the Massachusetts Association of Bilingual Educators, in my capacity as the official at the State Department of Education responsible for civil rights and urban education. I said then and I'd like to say again that my position has not changed—I'm strongly supportive of children learning in more than one language. I wrote the testimony for Commissioner Neil Sullivan nearly thirty years ago, when he testified in support of a Massachusetts bilingual law. The point we made in his testimony was that bilingual education would give a clear message that you can be smart in languages other than English and that bilingualism is a good thing.

I said at the MABE conference that if the school districts around the state were educating limited-English students and holding themselves accountable for helping these kids reach the same standards as other children, then I was happy for students to continue to be educated in two languages for twelve or fourteen years. I saw no need for kids ever to be exiting bilingual education.

But, I said, if limited-English kids are being segregated in separate programs where they only come together with other children for short lessons such as gym class, and if the bilingual students are not being held to the same academic standards but to a different set of expectations, then, as the civil rights official for the state, I'm going to get these kids out of those programs as quickly as possible.

So, I support bilingual education, and I have developed proposals for modifying Chapter 71-A (Transitional Bilingual Education law) in a way that would support bilingual education more adequately than it is supported now. I'm against separate bilingual programs. I think the day of separate bilingual programs has passed. I am for bilingual schools. I'm for schools where the principal has a staff, many or all of whom are bilingual, and who are thoroughly competent, and for schools which, with that kind of staff, organize themselves to serve all of the children in the school effectively—making use of both languages. Many of you have heard me say that it is extremely difficult to bring about changes that will make the school principal the person responsible for educating all the children in a school. There are enormous institutional pressures to maintain the separate structure of bilingual education.

One of the reasons it's difficult to get any changes in legislation is that each time there are proposals for change, there's a mobilization around the cry that an effort is being made to abolish bilingual education altogether. Again and again, my own children have brought home flyers from the Rafael Hernandez School saying that bilingual education is about to be abolished, though this has never been even a small possibility in the legislature.

I think we need to talk turkey about what kinds of concrete changes in Chapter 71-A will make school systems responsible for providing an appropriate amount of home language support but will also integrate these students and give them a strong education based on English. We know from the work of Steve Krashen [lead architect of the now-defunct bilingual education program in California] and others that we learn a language through using the language in learning other things. So we need instruction that is focused on using English to teach children other school subjects, just as my kids have been learning Spanish—not through doing Spanish lessons, but through doing their mathematics and their social studies and their language arts in Spanish.

I support the sort of thing that Mary Cazabon described earlier, the five or six different models operating in the Cambridge schools. All of these seemed to me appropriate alternatives to Transitional Bilingual Education. In every case, there seems to be some real determination both to have kids integrated and to hold them to high standards.

I suggested modified legislative language to change the current definition of bilingual education in the essay I originally wrote for the

Pioneer Institute. ("Rethinking Bilingual Education" appears on pages 4-31 of this volume.) The heart of it is to say that bilingual education is instruction in all the courses that are required in the schools, in English, and with the support of the native language for children of limited English-speaking ability; instruction in the reading and writing of the native language of the children of limited English-speaking ability; and in oral comprehension, speaking, reading, and writing of English.

Now, that may sound a lot like what we already have, but the difference is that I completely took out the idea that you select certain kids to be assigned to a separate program until some point at which you decide that those kids are ready to be removed from that program. The basis for many of my ideas is the work that I did in reviewing what other countries have chosen to do in educating their large immigrant populations. You may not be aware that in a number of other countries, the proportion of children from immigrant families is larger than the proportion in the United States. I've seen that, in country after country, there are two main practices. One is that as quickly as possible, often in the very first year, almost always after one year, these children are put in a regular class with other children. Fundamental. They do this in France, they do it in Sweden, they do it in Australia.

Second, in each of the dozen countries I have studied, except the United States, ongoing language and culture programs are made available, on a voluntary basis, as part of the regular school curriculum. For those children who choose this option, there is no implication that it is a remedial class or that they can't function in the regular school program. The schools do it because they think it is good education.

It is good education, and we need to move in that direction rather than continuing to fight in the trenches to keep things exactly as they have been for the last twenty-five years.

A State Legislator's Views on Bilingual Education Reform

Harold Lane: I could probably join a long list of people who said they're the only one here who knows very little about the program and the problem, but I won't do that.

It's interesting. You know you're getting to be one of the oldest in the room when the person who introduces you says, "many, many years," instead of giving an exact number.

In the last five minutes Richard Estrada [the conference keynote speaker] crystallized something that I believed for a long time, and that is that the Congress of the United States should bear a lot of the responsibility for the problems we're having because of its disdain for making a distinction between immigration policy on the one hand and immigrant policy. I think that's extremely important. It seems to me that some of the laws we have on bilingual education and non-English-speaking students in this country are driven by the rhetoric involved with the immigration policy. There seems to be such disdain of foreign people and people coming in without being able to speak English that it's created a real bind, and it's put up barriers that many of us find very difficult to climb over.

This issue of bilingual education certainly deserves our attention, but it's often been lost in the legislative shuffle, and in my committee in particular, as we try to monitor the implementation of the Education Reform Act, which is taking up most of our time. However, it is clearly an issue that must be carefully considered by the legislature, and I believe it will be, although I'm not sure it will be done as quickly as we might like.

One of the problems with this whole debate about bilingual education as I see it is that too often the different sides of the issue simply don't listen to each other, and thus we have built up two diametrically opposed groups who seem not to hear each other, who speak only to those who agree with them, and who vilify opposing viewpoints. It's a shame we have regressed to that in this society, because I think the kind of dialogue we have had today opened some doors and hopefully opened some ears and some eyes and really put the emphasis back where it belongs—on the individual child, the individual student's hopes and aspirations for the future.

I began by saying that I'm convinced that this issue must be addressed, if at all possible at the next session; however, I anticipate that we will probably first be taking up two items of an equally contentious nature, one being special education and the second being the need to develop a funding formula for education to take effect after the seven years of education reform initiative comes to a conclusion.

Thus, these two issues will be the primary ones we will focus on, but I think it will give us some time, using this conference as a starting point, to begin to meet with some people around the issue of bilingual education. Then, if we come up with changes in the law or make modifications to the law, they will be better thought out than if we had not had this opportunity.

At a minimum, I believe we must decide clearly what information we need to know to make good decisions about these programs, and frankly from my perspective on the Education Committee, this has been the real problem. Any bill, any legislation must both be clear about our goals and also clear about how we will measure those goals. Some states do this with annual tests of a child's development of language skills and academic skills.

While we would need to consider carefully the best ways of gathering such information, clearly this is step one. I believe strongly in data-driven public policy, and my frustration has been the multitude of studies that prove "opposite conclusions," and we've heard some of that today. We often receive in my office one persuasive report that bilingual programs are a disaster, followed immediately by a rebuttal or a separate study that shows precisely the opposite. This tends to confuse public policy and certainly confuses public policymakers, especially when every report proving bilingual education works seems to be sponsored by a proponent, and every report asserting its ineffectiveness comes to us from organized opponents. We need more people to look at this issue than those involved in the issue.

Moreover, even if one accepts the conclusions of some of these studies, they do not often tell us what we need most to know. Jay Greene's work, as an example, seems to say that some form of bilingual education is better than nothing, but gives little help in determining what kind of bilingual education to use and for how long. Frankly, his study wasn't intended to speak to those issues—of whether a cap should be placed on years in the program, or which kind of bilingual program might work best, et cetera.

These are important issues because in the last legislative session, at a hearing held on the subject, we asked the [state] Department of Education for an analysis of available statistics on bilingual education.

We felt that no matter what we decided should be our goals for the program, philosophically, we needed to know whether or not schools already are meeting these goals.

Guess what? There were no data available, and—this goes back to my experience as a school administrator—while school systems had loyally sent in material over the years, it was sitting in some closet somewhere, or some cellar, never having been analyzed. So while some data had been gathered by the Department of Education, it seems they had not been routinely analyzed or reported. We need to begin to ask the department to step to the fore and do this. My staff and I resolved at that time that the first part of any bilingual bill we ultimately develop would be an effort to bring bilingual education into the age of accountability, as, in fact, all schools and education programs are now facing.

Thus, if we also choose to add flexibility to the law and allow other types of programs to be offered, we can at least develop an internal ability at the department to monitor the effectiveness of each type of program in teaching English and preparing kids for learning school subjects and meeting statewide standards. That analysis should then be made available on a yearly basis to the board and to the legislature so that we can see for ourselves what is and isn't working.

One of the really sad parts of being an educator in Massachusetts is that we as the bedrock state for public education have done the lousiest job of doing anything coming close to educational research. Every other state in the Union seems to have an arm of research that looks into education matters, and we—who hold up Horace Mann, shout to the rafters that we are the end-all and be-all—don't have a research capability, and I hope we can correct that, too.

Any data that we gather will be without meaning unless we also know how we define our goals and determine what effective bilingual education means, and you've helped me with that today. People must know for what they are accountable in order to be truly held accountable. This requires some statement of our philosophy. So I should take a minute to give you mine, where I'm coming from.

Indeed, philosophy, whether people like it or not, is at the very heart of this debate, the more so because the per-pupil cost of bilingual education is not, on average, much higher than for regular education. That may come as a shocker to some, but it's true, although clearly that marginal cost adds up when a system has large numbers of students to provide for, or if the students stay for many years in the program. Essentially, unlike special education, where the per-pupil costs are crippling, the issue in bilingual education is as much and more about philosophy as about funding.

There is no question in my mind, no question at all, that all students must learn English well to survive and flourish in this, their country. This seems to me to be too basic a proposition to be denied, and all things equal, the swifter that is done the better. To send any child into life in the United States with an inadequate command of English is an act of deliberate cruelty, which will hinder the child's ability to get a good job, to achieve the so-called American dream, and to become an active citizen.

However, I do accept two caveats to that. First, proponents often argue that simply teaching English swiftly is insufficient if the students are not also given solid backing in academic subjects. As I think about this, we are all—at least my age—used to the Italian Americans and the German Americans and the French Americans telling us about the wonderful jobs that their grandparents did in emigrating to this country and how everybody now is getting an education.

But we've got to remember one thing that's very different about the immigration flood that came into this country back at the turn of the century. The schools weren't involved. People came to this country and they learned English in a job, and that was from age 12 on. So we didn't have this whole immediate problem of having to assimilate kids as quickly as we're trying to do now. Now the way is truly through education. That's a huge difference, and one I don't think any of us take into consideration enough.

So, to repeat, proponents of bilingual education often argue that simply teaching English swiftly is insufficient if the students are not also given solid backing in academic subjects. I'm sympathetic to this, at least in the upper grades. At the turn of the century, immigrants could survive simply learning some English and finding a laboring job that often provided decent money or at least enough to live on. That is much less the case now.

Indeed, one of the reasons for the Education Reform Act is precisely that we need all students to learn at a very high level if they're to get available jobs in the worldwide market. Thus, teaching English may be a minimum requirement of all schools, but proponents are not incorrect to note that it is equally crippling to send an immigrant student into the world with nothing but English skills.

I would note that I'm less persuaded by this argument when the students in question are in the early years of their learning and when the difference between social and academic language is narrow to nonexistent. I, for instance, see no particular reason, although I've talked to others who tell me there is, why a student of limited English proficiency in the second grade or the first grade or kindergarten, can't learn basic English words along with the student's English-speaking peers. Then when more technical language is needed in later years, learn that along with their peers as well, and learn it not in a separate classroom but with support in regular classrooms. With all the students, though, I think we do need to pay attention to the balance between English learning and academic content.

The second comment I would make is that we need to find a way to make the learning of English a goal without adding the vindictive and unnecessary goal of erasing these children's native language and culture. I say this because at the turn of the century, the time when many people like to brag that their grandfathers had to learn English, both the destruction of the old culture and the learning of the new were in fact joint goals of public policy, and I don't think they were good goals. That must change if we're to have effective bilingual education.

Indeed, in the modern economy, knowing a second language is an asset, not a burden, which is why one of the goals of education reform is precisely to make all students learn a foreign language as part of their studies. It seems to me it would be the height of hypocrisy to try to get a Hispanic student to forget Spanish only to insist the student learn a second language in high school if he/she wishes to graduate.

In one sense, we should see LEP students not merely as a challenge, but as a resource and an opportunity. We must ask not only how we can best teach these students English, but also how we can use their skills to help teach English-speaking children the foreign language we want them to acquire. In an ideal world, all students—Limited-English Proficient and English-speaking—would graduate from high school reading Shakespeare in English and Don Quixote in Spanish.

If it is cruel to send a student into the American economy without a good command of English, it is surely also a disadvantage to send him or her into a global economy without command of at least two languages. Thus, the second broad area in which I would make changes through any bilingual reform law is in giving local districts some flexibility in the choice of programs. I think we have got to come to that.

I agree with those who say that no conclusive reports have yet shown the complete failure or the total success of Transitional Bilingual Education. The fact that conclusive proof has not been presented of its superiority at least justifies some expansion of available program options. The governor's previous bill on this subject listed several additional options we might use in providing this service, including structured immersion and two-way bilingual programs. But I would suggest we try some pilot programs before we throw the baby out with the bath water.

As you can guess, I'm a strong supporter of not merely explicitly permitting such programs, but encouraging them as a way to make students in a school successfully bilingual. I had the privilege in the fall of 1998 of visiting the Underwood School in Newton. It's a fantastic school, which serves as a magnet for Newton's Chinese-speaking population. The school teaches bilingually for the early years in combination with an aggressive English instruction, then combine both Limited English Proficient and English-speaking students to teach each other in their native language.

I want to tell you, the pride on the faces of the native Chinese-speaking students who suddenly saw they had something to teach their peers was inspiring, and they learn English much more aggressively when they realize they're not being asked to learn English as an insult, but as a benefit to them, and that the value of their original language was not being discounted.

I was also impressed recently by a Heritage Foundation article recently about the success of the El Paso school system where the superintendent, Mr. Trujillo, has a schoolwide mission statement that all students should graduate fluently bilingual, which excites and involves parents and students. This district's ultimate intent is to do this through two-way bilingual programs and I think the commonwealth should consider some of those.

The second model the previous governor recommended using in the legislation he submitted was structured immersion, about which I personally would want a great deal more information. As mentioned above, I am more sympathetic to such an approach in the early grades. I am persuaded from observation that young children learn languages very quickly indeed, and it makes more sense to try to speed up language acquisition in those grades.

Again, last year I saw a superb French immersion program in the town of Milton, which was teaching students fluency in French in the early grades. At least to someone who doesn't speak French, the students appeared to have great fluency. However, my sense would be that any flexibility with regard to so-called structured immersion approaches should be initially limited to some pilot programs in the early grades, and as we collect data about the success or failures of these programs, we can consider expanding them.

If we have clear proof of the success of such approaches, we can make better decisions about which kinds of programs would be allowed in greater number; and if we had proof that those programs work, it might help comfort parents and advocates concerned about change.

Let me close by stating why we did not pass the bill given us by the governor, or a version of it, in the last session. Aside from the fact that our emphasis was on the continued implementation of education reform and the charter school expansion bill and the special education reform bill, there were also several specific concerns. We had received commentary from the civil rights office of the U.S. Department of Education, which oversees compliance, and we couldn't ignore this.

First, the civil rights office indicated to us that a simple three-year cutoff would be unacceptable under its current policy if that cutoff meant students who needed services were denied them. Seems obvious. There might be two possible responses to this. First, we could explore whether a cutoff combined with appropriate supports in the classroom would be acceptable, thus ending segregation and separate classrooms, but still providing supports to those who need them. Second, we could use the results of any accountability system to determine which schools needed the most improvement in their bilingual program and ask the Massachusetts Department of Education to target those schools for technical assistance to restructure their programs for greater effectiveness.

Last year, we found that many more schools than we thought had high percentages of students leaving bilingual programs on time, in three years. It may be that our initial effort should be on the most egregious cases of long-term placement and on providing assistance to them to improve and better carry on their programs.

REFLECTIONS OF A SCHOOL SUPERINTENDENT—QUINCY, MASSACHUSETTS

Eugene Creedon: It's a pleasure for me to be here today and to have been a part of the program since early morning, and I certainly want to thank Rosalie for asking me to be a participant. I'm not quite sure if I really belong with the panel, or the people who have spoken, but I will try.

I was introduced as having spent all of my professional career in the Quincy Public Schools and educated in the Quincy Public Schools. I would also like to point out that so was the chairman [Harold Lane, Chairman of the House Education Committee]. At least part of his education—a good part of it, two-thirds of it—was in the Quincy Public Schools, and I think the principal of your old grammar school is here in this audience, and he might want to check things out. She probably has your records back to those days. Didn't you to go to the Wollaston?

Representative Lane: No, I went to Montclair.

Mr. Creedon: I take it back. But I'm really delighted to be here and to participate. Like Tom Doluisio, I'm a superintendent and sometimes you begin to think, well, you're the person who probably knows the least about what's happening in your programs. I have the same kind of feelings that he shared with you on that score. I'm not the person who's there on the front lines day by day. I do think, though, that I have a healthy knowledge of what's happening in our programs.

I want to state a few of my beliefs right from the very start. First of all, I believe strongly in transitioning our LEP students to English as soon as possible, and that means as appropriately as possible. As other speakers have said so often, the key to success for all students is to become proficient in English. Second, I also have strong, very strong, feelings that we have in our schools a serious responsibility to do whatever we can to assist our students to preserve and maintain their own language, their first language. Nevertheless, our primary responsibility is to provide transition to the full use of English.

Another of my beliefs, which I want to state emphatically, is that we as educators must integrate culture into the regular curriculum. To say that we don't have time to teach culture or that it is not our responsibility certainly is not the way we approach our students and their families in the Quincy Public Schools.

The traditional approach of celebrating the holidays is a primary example of bringing an understanding of cultural differences into the lives of our children. My wife is a first-grade teacher and I recently said to her, "What would you do throughout first grade if you didn't have the holidays?" So much excitement is brought into the lives of the young learners by integrating the literature, reading, and math lessons of the day with the holidays and seasonal events. Is this not teaching culture?

Teaching culture is not only routinely included in the primary grades but is also a practice that continues throughout the grades and into the classrooms of our high schools. An example of what I am talking about is that today in the City of Quincy, we celebrate the birthday of John Adams, second President of our country. A significant group of students will be at the Church of the Presidents in Quincy Square to assist and to participate in the ceremony of placing the presidential wreath on the tomb of John Adams. I believe that participation of students in civic observances inculcates into the heart and soul of our students something of Quincy's unique culture and heritage, whether the students be first generation Asians or Hispanics, or Caucasians who can trace their ancestry to Quincy's founding families. To me, this is culture and our students of today, no matter what their primary language is, must be as proud of the contributions of John Adams and his work as a founding father as Quincy children in earlier generations.

A number of years ago, I was principal of the Parker Elementary School in North Quincy. I was principal there for eleven years; at that time it was kindergarten through fifth grade. We had a very growing and strong Greek population; about 17 percent of the school population were children of Greek parents and were Greek-speaking youngsters. It was actually at the very beginning of our ESL program when we began to understand the need to support these youngsters in the regular classrooms.

One little guy, Savas, was coming out the side door and getting ready to go home. It was a windy March day, and in the class, as an art project, they made little leprechauns. He had his leprechaun, and a gust of wind came along and took that leprechaun and sent it flying down the street, and he looked up at me—he always called me Mr. Creeger—he said, "Hey, Mr. Creeger, there goes my Irish!" I thought, you aren't kidding, there goes your Irish.

Those kind of cultural things are very much a part of what we do, so I believe that we do teach culture, we do integrate it into our lessons. It is through teaching culture that we help our students understand each other and help our parents understand the practices of someone from a different culture. They need to work together. They need to become a body of people that can work for the good of the school, and if the parents are not accepting of the culture of a neighbor or a group of neighbors, then you don't have that full life of the school going on, which I think is so critically important for a healthy school.

Our school system enrolls about 9,000 students. We have a minority population of about 27 percent. Our limited-English proficient primarily are Asian students, most being Chinese and Vietnamese, and some Cambodians. Our next language minority group is Arabic, but it's the Asian population to whom we offer a transitional bilingual program in Chinese at the elementary, middle, and high school levels; a Vietnamese program at the elementary, middle, and high school levels; and an ESL support system throughout the school system.

I think we have about 823 students in our TBE/ESL (Transitional Bilingual Education/English as a Second Language) program. Of that number, approximately eighty youngsters are in Transitional Bilingual Education programs. We have a very active Asian parents group that meets once a month. What I have found out is that if a son or daughter qualifies for a transitional bilingual program, parents are very willing to accept it—if it's within their neighborhood school. If it means leaving the neighborhood school, being bused someplace else, the parents are not quite as receptive—they really want their children to stay in the neighborhood school.

Two years ago, we had an audit on a number of our programs by the Massachusetts Department of Education, and the Office of Civil Rights (OCR) joined in the audit of our bilingual and ESL programs. I just couldn't quite seem to get that point through to those people. Not to the Department of Education people, but the OCR people—that our parents were doing what Caucasian parents do. They want the school that they can see, the school that's in their neighborhood, the school that they know, the school that they can walk to, the school that Mrs. Smith's kids are going to. They want their children in that school.

In a district like Quincy, with centralized programs for budgetary purposes, obviously we don't have a bilingual program in every school. It means that some people, if they want the bilingual program, are going to have to leave their neighborhood school. Many of them choose not to. They say, "No thank you, we're not going to leave our neighborhood school." Here is where we need flexibility with the ESL/TBE regulations and the law. We asked for a waiver to allow us to develop a system of multi-lingual classrooms throughout the system, site-based, that would allow us to provide meaningful support in each one of our schools for our rapidly increasing number of English language learners. The waiver was rejected, and we have implemented the TBE programs as required. But remember, many children will not get the language support we could have given them because our budget is supporting TBE programs, with only limited resources going to multilingual classes.

One of the things I like to talk about is to refer to the fact that our first superintendent of schools was Colonel Francis Parker. Colonel Parker was superintendent of the Quincy school district from 1875 to 1880. John Dewey, in Parker's later life, was to refer to him as the father of progressive education in the United States. By the way, Parker spent a long part of his career in Chicago where he worked with Dewey.

When Parker was asked as a superintendent to describe his success in Quincy and the method he used there, he said that there never was a Quincy method or a Quincy system, unless we agree to call the Quincy method a spirit of study and the Quincy system one of everlasting change. I feel very strongly that this same spirit is present in all that we do today.

We don't have all the answers, we don't know what program works best, we don't know what organization is necessarily the best. It's a combination of things, but we need to keep studying and we need to keep looking for that research that's going to help us in the decision-making process. That's what we believe in, as a school system, in charting the future. Continually concerned about what the research can tell us about the best way to enhance the education of the English language learner.

The second thing that Parker talked about is everlasting change. There will constantly and continually be things that we need to do differently; new approaches must be tried. What I want to repeat as a superintendent is the frustration of trying to be flexible and looking for that flexibility. I don't fault the Department of Education. I think it was interpreting the law to the letter, but it set us back somewhat. We were forced to develop a program for four students, a teacher, and an aide, while three other schools got nothing additional because we couldn't try our model.

Again, I stress that I believe firmly that our mission, our goal, is to enhance the transition to English. We want to respect and retain and do everything we can for that first language, to promote it, so that it becomes a part of their life, of the lives of our children. Respect for cultural diversity is extremely important. It is a thread that must be a part of the very fabric of our schools.

CHELSEA SUPERINTENDENT URGES MORE FLEXIBILITY IN STATE BILINGUAL LAW

Douglas Sears: The last time I was in this room was ten years ago, when I first came to Boston University. It's been a good long busy ten years, and in fact when I come up for my ten-year anniversary, I'm going to ask to be given a clock for twenty, because it wasn't mentioned that, before going to Chelsea, I was chief of staff for John Silber.

It is always interesting to hear the statistics for other districts in the greater Boston area. In measurements such as the percentage of children in a district who are not native speakers of English, we've done a grand flip-flop; the so-called majorities are the minorities. Chelsea is where America begins. As of today, we have only 1,708 students from English-speaking homes. That is slightly less than one-third of the 5,800 students currently registered in Chelsea schools. The total enrollment is also growing rapidly as families stream in from all over the world. Most recently, we've seen growth spurts in the numbers of Bosnians, Kurds, and Somalis. We are magnificently diverse.

I don't propose to describe all the different things we do, because really what we do in Transitional Bilingual Education is defined by law, so we do what the law calls for. I'll simply say that the beauty of this panel is it forced me to read Charlie Glenn's paper. I think Charlie has some very useful things to say about the construction of the Transitional Bilingual Education law and how it might be changed. As a comment on this whole debate, I would like to offer the suggestion that the great debate about the merits of Transitional Bilingual Education programs versus immersion in its various moderated and modified incarnations cannot be resolved by comparing empirical research studies. Fundamentally, the epistemologies of these studies are flawed.

You really cannot draw meaningful and instructive conclusions and make prescriptions on the basis of empirical studies. Mountains of data will not resolve the questions we need to be asking. The most important question seems to be: What is the most effective way for children to acquire a second language? One axis of the debate centers on whether children need to learn each new skill or subject in their primary language before "transferring" it to English. Let me offer three comments on this question.

Historically, one can find numerous examples of people at all levels of academic proficiency who immigrate to a new country and continue their development in the common language of the host country. I know people who study abroad and learn about unfamiliar subjects in a second language. Others report that it is actually easier to learn a third language through the medium of the second. For example, one native English speaker I know studied the Russian language while living in Germany. She found that working from a second language (German) to Russian forced her to think more clearly about the grammar and syntax of Russian. I don't see why this couldn't be applied to the study of other subjects.

Second, the goal for language-minority students in our public schools is to get these children thinking and working in English—not simply to be able to transfer or translate a body of knowledge from their primary language to English. They must be able to continue their development, in academics and in professional and civic life, in English. Children who do not acquire this skill will not be able to take advantage of many of the opportunities for further growth.

My third thought on this subject is that the conception of language which is implied by the word "transfer," as if language were only a vehicle for transferring knowledge from one language to another, may be seriously limiting. I hear this sort of talk about literacy as well. The current jargon refers to language as a "code," reading as "decoding," and spelling as "encoding." A danger I see in this terminology is that language is implicitly viewed as something foreign and intimidating, even cryptic. Language is, however, essential to being human. Can we ask that children take responsibility for their words if language is viewed as only accurate or inaccurate "codes" for what one truly means? Language should be taken more seriously—it is the only objective method by which we can communicate. For one, our legal system is obviously based upon the accuracy of words, which are the only concrete evidence we have of the lawmakers' intent.

Another quarrel I have with the term "code" is that it implies that learning to speak, read, and write English is an option when, in fact, it is absolutely necessary for full participation as an American citizen. Learning about life in the community in which one lives is not an option, although learning a particular "code" would be. By thinking of language only as a code, we avoid turning inward to understand how we actually speak and write, and we do not understand the relationship between our intentions and our expressions.

I do believe that there are some fundamental mechanisms by which people learn a second language, and that these can be described, categorized, and tabulated in research studies. These data will be useful for English-speaking students as well. In fact, one of the goals of the Massachusetts Frameworks—that every student will learn a second language—requires that we learn more about second-language learning in general.

But we must recognize that there are many variables involved in the most avowedly empirical studies—the relationship of a child's native language and culture to English and to American culture, the parents' level of education, the child's age, the child's level of education in his or her primary language in the land of origin, the quality and duration of formal schooling, the attitude toward cultural and linguistic assimilation and, perhaps most important, the quality of the instruction in the classroom.

Many children find a home in Chelsea after years of living in refugee camps. Many of these children are not accustomed to structured environments, let alone prepared to study in an American classroom. While it is important to define the factors in general that lead to students' success in acquiring a second language, it is even more useful to rely on the knowledge gained from particular cases in planning the strategies employed in teaching a group of language-minority students.

I've noticed in Chelsea that some of our very best teaching takes place in Spanish. We have some really marvelous, idealistic bilingual teachers who teach beautifully in different languages. Since we offer so many different bilingual programs, we have to recruit very creatively to overcome the obstacles posed by the commonwealth's antediluvian certification system. It could be argued that were the same gifted and talented teachers to immerse their students in English, these teachers would produce extraordinary results. I would find it challenging to design a sound research study that could isolate the variable of teaching effectiveness from the variable of language. I would also judge the quality and tone of teaching in the classroom as perhaps the most crucial variable in accounting for the success of children.

We have found some very able, bright teachers who are doing a great job in the classroom. As an example of the kinds of people we have recruited, we have on staff a Bosnian bilingual teacher who holds a degree from the University of Saravejo and who was at one time the Bosnian women's national speed-skating champion. She must be imparting the drill she learned around the rink to her elementary school students. I once observed five of her students reading a short book out loud to each other. Some of the children were very new to the United States and had a good deal of trouble sounding out the English words. Each time they (laboriously) made it to the end of the story, they would turn back to the first page and begin all over again— time after time, on their own initiative.

To address the issue of bilingual education, I think we need to step back and talk to some good philosophers about the nature of language acquisition and about the methods of measuring it. My editorial for the day would be to suggest that scholars rely not only on the empirical surveys, but try to further our understanding of how languages are learned.

Bad theory is saved by good practice. A policy that depends upon the good sense of the implementers to subvert it entirely is one that needs reform. The Commonwealth resorts to magic to meet the task defined by law—instead of a wand, numerology. There are accepted mechanisms by which all people learn a second language, and these can be explicated. These techniques will be useful for English-speaking students as well. In fact, the goal of the Massachusetts Frameworks is that every student will graduate from high school with a knowledge of two languages.

My advice is partly based on my own experience learning a foreign language for my work in the Foreign Service. One of my big frustrations was that the taxpayers spent a lot of money to teach me German. I then went to Switzerland, where the Swiss officials speak such elegant English that they refuse to speak German to you. When we would pull up at an Esso station and say, "Fill'er up," in German, the attendant would say, "What'll it be, regular?" Just like that, in English. The guy would do the same thing in Spanish for the Spanish diplomats and French for the French diplomats, and even in Russian. I thought that was a pretty respectable level of language education.

In Chelsea, much of the impetus to value the study of language comes from Boston University. In the early grades, we have established an excellent two-way bilingual program. We provide sheltered English classrooms, and we have concentrated much time and energy on improving our methods of teaching English as a Second Language. I think in the time I've been there, we've seen a greater rigor in teaching, right across the board.

I, for my part, would like to see in the bilingual law a flexibility that allows us to move more quickly into English. I think the current law is too inflexible, but I'm not going to spend a lot of time on it. My own experience with language in Chelsea is the sooner you can move kids into English, the better. It does not mean that they should not be taught other languages or that you should not cherish the native language, and we have more than 4,000 students who bring to us such languages as Amharic, Mandinka, Korean, not to mention Bosnian and Somali. We're teaching in a lot of languages in Chelsea because our numbers drive us there. It's fun, it's interesting, but I think the law is restrictive. In my opinion, it would be nice to have more flexibility, and I very much like Charlie Glenn's suggestions in his article.

Finally, a comment about the politics of bilingual education. In the time I've been in Chelsea, I've come to think that there are two worlds. I inhabit a world of parents and kids, and then somewhere out there, there's the *Boston Globe* and a world of activists and ideologues. This is a community in which the majority of parents speak Spanish. When the Boston University/Chelsea contract came up for renewal—and you should know that the reputation of the university is well known, and Dr. Silber is highly visible—nobody turned out to oppose this renewal effort, nobody came to the meetings. The meetings were well publicized in many languages; we invited lots of comment.

It's a town where people turn out if they're angry. What turns parents out in Chelsea—I can tell you because they come in and yell and call me good names and bad names—is problems with busing, problems with toilet paper missing in the bathrooms, problems with discipline, problems with safety. As far as I can tell, what real parents want is safe schools and a good education. They don't want you to get too ideological about it; they want you to do a good job. And they do want, I'm very confident of this, their kids to know English very well. I think their aspirations for their children are that they want kids to know English very well and to do well in school. These parents don't get drawn into the ideological arguments. Once we understood in Chelsea the advocate game and the political game and started to, frankly, ignore it, the city became a very quiet place on that political front. Hundreds of parents turn out for the open-house evenings at our schools now. So it's not a problem attracting parents: parents come when they're interested in what's going on in the building.

I think one other thing we have done here is instructive, and I'd like people to know about it. I'm grateful to the state for the Education Reform Law which gives superintendents a lot of authority to appoint principals. I've exercised it. I appointed a high school principal I borrowed from John Silber's staff, Lincoln Tamayo. He's bilingual, he's a lawyer, he has an unorthodox certification. He's building a good high school, test scores are up, attendance is up, discipline is much better. Parents turn out for his open-house evenings in droves— one of the things he does well. And he'll tell you his Spanish is not perfect, but he's in very close communication with parents. He gets on the local cable TV station and does spots in Spanish.

We want parents to feel comfortable in our buildings. We've opened our doors. The last three principals I have appointed are all bilingual in Spanish. Each new principal has made an effort to build a bilingual front office staff, because we want parents in the building and comfortable with our staffs. Any time I'm recruiting and I see a candidate who has some range in language, I try to hire that person. I'm looking for language capacity because I like what it says about intelligence and depth of knowledge. It gives a much better understanding of how kids acquire language, and it just gives us the ability to relate to parents.

I'll end with this thought. I believe strongly that freed of the confines of the Commonwealth's wrong-headed TBE law and regulations, we could do significantly more to improve instruction and create genuine opportunities for Chelsea's children and young people.

APPENDIX 1

MYSTERY ON THE BILINGUAL EXPRESS: A CRITIQUE OF THE THOMAS AND COLLIER STUDY

Christine H. Rossell
Boston University

EXECUTIVE SUMMARY

Perhaps no other "yet to be released" report has been quoted so much or so often as the so-called Collier Study. In 1995, approximately two years before the report was completed, Virginia Collier was holding public meetings at which she disseminated a five-page summary of her "study"—two pages of text, two pages of line graphs, and a one-page list of program definitions. In no time, the Collier Study had become another factoid in the controversy over bilingual education. Even though no one had actually read it, the report was being cited everywhere as proof that bilingual education, particularly two-way bilingual education, was superior to all other programs for Limited-English Proficient (LEP) children.

Some two years later, the complete report has finally been issued.[1] Although 96 pages long, it contains no more data on the findings of the study than the same two charts in the original press release. There are no tables at all, and the few other charts in the study are merely illustrations of the authors' theories. In fact, this report consists primarily of theories of bilingual education and criticism of the scientific method.

---

[1] "School Effectiveness for Language Minority Students" (National Clearinghouse on Bilingual Education Resource Collection Series, No. 9, December 1997). This document can be downloaded from the National Clearinghouse for Bilingual Education web page at www.ncbe.gwu.edu/ncbepubs.

The study analyzes eleven grades of achievement data over a fifteen-year period from 1982 to 1996 in six elementary school programs for LEP children. The programs analyzed are: (1) two-way bilingual education; (2) one-way developmental (or maintenance) bilingual programs; (3) transitional bilingual education with ESL taught through academic content; (4) transitional bilingual education taught "traditionally," with ESL taught "traditionally"; (5) ESL content (also called sheltered or structured immersion); and (6) ESL pullout. These programs were implemented in five medium-to-large urban and suburban school districts across the U.S. Beginning with 700,000 student records, Thomas and Collier selected 42,317 students with four years or more of data and achievement growth with "some generalizability." They discarded results they thought were "unique" to a school district. This procedure of picking and choosing achievement patterns represents a large step backward from the goal of scientific inquiry, which is to achieve results that are objective and verifiable.

The Thomas and Collier study has several more serious problems. First, it uses a methodology—a simple descriptive cohort analysis—that is unscientific and that can produce misleading results. The method is unscientific because each grade consists of different students—eleven grades are studied, but most students have only four years of achievement data—and there is no statistical control for pre-treatment differences that existed before the students were in the program. The achievement of students enrolled in elementary school programs is compared to the achievement of different students in junior high and high school who were apparently in similar programs in elementary school. Even if Thomas and Collier had followed the same students over time, this study would be unscientific because it is not possible to determine the effect of a program that a student participated in many years ago without controlling for the student's individual characteristics and the characteristics of his or her current school and program.

Using the same methodology that Thomas and Collier used, I demonstrate (in the complete review) that it is mathematically possible that the average achievement for a bilingual program could show an increase from fourth- through eleventh-grade (eight years) even though each individual student in the program had a decline over their four years of testing. This phenomenon is well known among social scientists trained in statistics, and it is why the methodology used by Thomas and Collier—a simple descriptive cohort analysis—is considered unscientific.

Almost as disturbing as these methodological problems is the nearly complete lack of data in this study. Although 96 pages long, the final report contains no more data on the findings of the study than the five-page 1995 press release. There is also no information on any of the characteristics of any of these programs, the children enrolled in them, the schools in which they reside, or the school districts. We literally know nothing about these school districts and their schools other than the fact that there are five of them and they are "moderate-to-large, urban and suburban school systems from all over the U.S." Even the programs are defined only in generalities that could apply to any program of that type in any district.

Thomas and Collier held "focus groups" with bilingual/ESL teachers and resource staff to determine the quality and type of program implemented in their school districts over the fifteen years of the study. There is only one brief paragraph describing this procedure. We do not know what questions were asked, what topics were discussed, when these focus groups were held over the fifteen-year period, how many were held, or how the information obtained in this process helped to define programs and evaluate the "atmosphere." Focus groups are not a substitute for observations of classrooms to determine how "bilingual" a program is. Nor are they a substitute for hard data on program quality. These data might include: class size, teacher qualifications, percentage of English used in instruction at each grade, racial composition of the classroom and school, percentage of students eligible for free or reduced lunch in the classroom and school, percentage classified LEP, standardized achievement test scores, English proficiency tests, reclassification rates, non-testing rates, and so forth. None of this is in the report, and there is no promise of it in future reports.

Whereas federal grant reports typically have dozens of tables, charts, and appendices on the characteristics of the sample, methodology, and statistical analysis representing one-half to two-thirds of the study, the Thomas and Collier report has only two line graphs on the findings of the study, representing 1 percent of the report. As noted above, most of the 96 pages are on theories of bilingual education and criticism of the scientific method.

To summarize, the Thomas and Collier study suffers from two serious flaws. First, it employs a methodology—a simple descriptive cohort analysis—that can produce misleading results; Thomas and Collier have admitted that they selected only the trends which they thought "assumed some generalizability." Second, there are virtually no data in this study. Thomas and Collier explain very little about their methodology, and they present no information on the characteristics of their sample nor any statistical analyses. In twenty-five years of reading technical reports, I have never seen a federally funded empirical research study with so little information in it. This report thus represents a new low in federal grant reporting.

APPENDIX 2

EL PASO PROGRAMS FOR ENGLISH LANGUAGE LEARNERS: A FOLLOW-UP STUDY

Russell Gersten, Scott Baker, and Thomas Keating
Eugene Research Institute, University of Oregon

EXECUTIVE SUMMARY

The READ Institute commissioned a follow-up study on limited-English students who have been in the El Paso, Texas, public schools since the first grade. These students, who were enrolled in two different programs in the elementary grades—some in the Spanish bilingual classroom, some in the English immersion classes—are now assessed at the high school level to determine the effects of these different programs on academic performance. Professors Gersten, Baker, and Keating found that differences in academic performance between the two groups in reading, math and writing are not dramatic or significant in grades 10–12. A predominant theory of bilingual education is that, in the long term, students who receive five to seven years of native language instruction will surpass students who are taught only in English from the first grade. This prediction is not at all supported by the results of the El Paso follow-up study.

First El Paso Study
In 1992, the READ Institute commissioned and published the results of the first El Paso study conducted by Professors Russell Gersten of the University of Oregon, John Woodard of the University of Puget Sound, and Susan Schneider of the El Paso School District. The purpose of this study was to provide a comparison of the results of the district's established Spanish bilingual program with the newer English immersion program which stresses intensive early English language academic instruction. Ten schools were examined. Five enrolled English learners in the immersion program, where all school subjects were taught in English from the first day of school, with 30–90 minutes a day of Spanish instruction. The other five schools offered English learners the Spanish bilingual program, where all subjects were taught in the native language (Spanish), through grade 5 or 6 with a 30–60 minute English lesson daily.

By grade 5, 99 percent of the immersion students had "graduated" from the English language program and were participating in mainstream classrooms, while 40 percent of the students in the comparison group were still in the Spanish bilingual program in the sixth grade. The study found that by the end of seventh grade, students who had been taught in the native language for the first four years had achieved comparable academic results to those who had received instruction in English immersion classes.

Follow-up High School Evaluation
To measure the long-term effects of these two programs, the current follow-up study examined the achievement data of those students in the original groups who are now in El Paso high schools. The purpose of the follow-up evaluation was to deter-

mine whether there were effects on high school achievement for English language learners due to the type of instruction received in grades 1 through 5. Reading, math, and writing performances were compared between the two groups. The original study included 111 students in the English immersion program and 117 students in the transitional bilingual education program. Due to attrition from both groups, i.e., students moving out of El Paso or dropping out before completing high school, (19.8 percent in the English immersion sample and 26.5 percent in the transitional bilingual education sample), the follow-up study sample included 89 students from the early English immersion program and 86 students from the Transitional Bilingual Education program.

Scores on the Texas Assessment of Academic Skills (TAAS) test, which all students are required to pass in order to graduate, and which include reading, math, and writing components, were analyzed for all students in the sample from 1994 to 1996. Students may take these tests up to eight times. Each student's highest scores were analyzed. According to Gersten et al.,   ". . . the TAAS represented the best source available to analyze differences between English-language learners in the English immersion and Transitional Bilingual Education programs because of the importance of the test." Academic achievement comparisons were made based on standardized, multiple-choice tests in reading, math, and writing, as well as a performance measure of student writing. Overall grade point averages were examined to compare differences between the two groups. Percentile rank scores were analyzed to compare the two groups to students throughout Texas.

Importance of Findings

Results of statistical analyses of achievement for the two groups of students showed no significant differences between the English immersion group and the transitional bilingual education group on reading, math, or writing measures.

Professors Gersten, Baker, and Keating's longitudinal study is important in the research literature for these reasons:

- students who started school with limited fluency in English had the same socioeconomic status shared the same native

language and ethnicity were enrolled in the same urban
school district participated in entirely different programs
• data collection took place over a 10-year period

The most important findings:

• Long years of native language instruction do not lead to higher
levels of academic performance for limited-English students.
• Early immersion in English does not lead to lower self-esteem or higher dropout rates for Latino students.
• Initial reading skills can be learned in a second language
(English); initial reading and writing in Spanish do not result in better literacy skills in English.

Conclusions

Some findings of this study are disappointing. The El Paso high
school longitudinal data from this current evaluation indicate that
the overall level of performance is low for all English language learners in both the English immersion group and the transitional bilingual education group when compared to native English speakers.
Gersten, Baker, and Keating point to the effect of other factors, such
as low-socioeconomic strata, and suggest that there is a need for
"... reforming and restructuring the middle and high school curriculum for minority students." The fact that no significant differences were found between the bilingual (English) immersion and
Spanish bilingual program effects on high school achievement, when
dramatically different results were reported up to grade 7, raises
new questions for further research. Another factor that was found
to have a possible impact is the effect of the type of instructional
approach used to teach reading to English language learners in the
elementary grades. When researchers of this current study sought
to explore the impact of instructional variables on English language
learning, they found very few studies that addressed the components of effective instruction.

The policy implications of the findings of the El Paso study support
the call for changes in bilingual education. The El Paso findings
disprove the notion that meaningful literacy instruction in English
cannot begin until students have had many years of native language

instruction. After twenty-five years of research, little evidence has been found to support Transitional Bilingual Education as the preferred method of teaching limited-English students.

Gersten, Baker, and Keating conclude that "...these findings fail to support the widely held belief that increased native language instruction throughout the seven years of elementary school will lead to better long-term outcomes than a much more rapid introduction of English language instruction. For that reason, we urge policymakers to seriously question their investment in an approach that has no empirical support."

APPENDIX 3

THE LABOR MARKET EFFECTS OF BILINGUAL EDUCATION AMONG HISPANIC WORKERS

Mark Hugo Lopez
University of Maryland

Marie T. Mora
New Mexico State University

EXECUTIVE SUMMARY

Recent growth of the language-minority population has shifted the linguistic distribution in the United States. For example, the U.S. decennial censuses report that the population share of residents aged 5 years and older who speak a non-English language at home rose from 11 percent to 13.8 percent (from approximately 23 million to

31.5 million individuals) between 1980 and 1990. Moreover, the portion of language minorities who report speaking English either "not well" or "not at all" increased from 18.3 percent to 21 percent during this time. Social scientists have consistently shown that English fluency promotes academic achievement, higher earnings, and occupational sorting in the U.S. But little attention has focused on the educational vehicles by which Limited-English Proficient (LEP) students acquire English skills. These changing linguistic demographics indicate that U.S. schools face the task of instructing larger numbers of children with a limited knowledge of English. Indeed, recent estimates suggest that LEP students represent at least 5 percent of all K-12 public school children.

Over the past twenty-five years, schools have responded to the growing numbers of LEP children by instituting a variety of bilingual education programs. Such programs, however, are costly. Recent data report that between $2 billion and $3 billion are spent per year on special educational services for LEP students at the state and local level. Additionally, despite the fact that the U.S. Department of Education receives federal on-budget funds for bilingual education programs, widespread disagreement exists over its relative effectiveness.

Typically, studies on the effectiveness of bilingual education programs concentrate on two questions: Do bilingual education programs improve the English fluency of Limited-English Proficient students? And do the programs provide opportunities for students to progress academically at the same rate as their English-speaking peers?

However, one important (and often overlooked) facet of bilingual education is its potential influence on the future labor market outcomes of LEP students. Using data from the Restricted-Use High School and Beyond (HSB) data set, our study compared the earnings between Hispanic workers by immigrant status who received bilingual education at some point during their schooling careers and their otherwise similar English-immersed peers.

In 1980, the National Center for Education Statistics (NCES) sponsored HSB to obtain a national longitudinal data set of high school students who were either sophomores or seniors; these students

Table 1

Regression Adjusted Earnings Differences Between Bilingual Education Participants and Non-Participants by Immigrant Status
Hispanics Only
(weighted differences)

| | Bilingual Education | | |
	Participants	Non-Participants	Approximate % Difference
Immigrants	$18,478	$24,200	–31%**
N=216			
Second Generation	$18,886	$23,513	–24.5%**
N=253			
Third Generation	$17,292	$17,516	–1.3%
N=645			
Full Sample	$17,294	$17,040	1.0%
N=1,298			

were followed up in 1982, 1984, 1986, and, most recently for the sophomores, in 1992. HSB contains a wealth of information on students' background and language use, academic and high school characteristics, and work experience by 1992. Our sample of interest includes the 1,298 Hispanic workers reporting earnings in 1992 who could have been classified as LEP at some point in their youth, and hence were potential candidates for bilingual education.

This study identifies bilingual education participants by using the HSB information on whether the individuals took English classes for non-English speakers, or if they had received instruction in other academic subjects (such as mathematics) in a minority language in grades 1–6, 7–9, and 10–12. Although this measure of bilingual education may not be perfectly defined because of its broad scope, it is the closest approximation available given the information in HSB, and represents some of the only data available on the link between participation in bilingual education programs and labor market earnings.

Controlling for an extensive list of personal, school, and labor market characteristics, we empirically estimate an ordinary least squares model to analyze the relationship between bilingual education and earnings. On the surface, the effect of bilingual education on earnings appears statistically indistinguishable from zero for the Hispanic sample. However, when partitioning the sample by generation of immigration, striking results appear. Specifically, we find that, when adjusting for background factors, first generation Hispanics (immigrants) who participated in bilingual education earned approximately $18,500 in 1991 while first generation Hispanic non-bilingual education participants earned approximately $25,000. That is a statistically significant difference (approximately 35 percent less) between bilingual education participants and their otherwise similar English-immersed peers. Moreover, we observe a similar negative (but smaller in magnitude) effect of bilingual education on the earnings of second generation workers. Among third generation Hispanics, bilingual education does not appear significantly related to income (see Table 1).

These results are alarming because immigrants conceptually have the most to gain from bilingual education. Yet, conditional on a number of background characteristics, recent Hispanic immigrants who went through bilingual education programs are earning much less ten years after high school than Hispanic immigrants who did not receive any bilingual education. While there are other potential explanations for the differences we observe, at a national level our results suggest that bilingual education programs as they are currently implemented may widen the socioeconomic gap between LEP and English-proficient populations over time.

Schooling programs designed for LEP students have become increasingly important in light of the current demographic shift away from monolingual English populations in this country. Policymakers should be aware that instructional programs designed for Limited-English Proficient students enacted today will affect the economic opportunities for increasing segments of the population far into the twenty-first century.

Notes:
    The average age of sample members is 28.
    Starred differences are statistically significant at the 5 percent level. Data comes from High School and Beyond, Restricted Use Sample, 1992 follow-up.

Individual grouping totals do not equal full sample size because we were unable to identify immigrant status for some
sample members.
The above figures are estimated using an ordinary least
squares model, controlling for potential experience, education, personal characteristics, and the quality of a student's
high school in 1980.
Further research is planned to examine the differences between first, second, and third generation immigrants' earning
levels.

APPENDIX 4

FOUR-YEAR LONGITUDINAL REPORT FOR THE ENGLISH ACQUISITION PROGRAM IN THE BETHLEHEM, PENNSYLVANIA, AREA SCHOOL DISTRICT

Ann Goldberg
Bethlehem Area School District

EXECUTIVE SUMMARY

In the fall of 1993, the city of Bethlehem, Pennsylvania, made a dar-
ing educational decision. The local school district voted to replace a
Spanish bilingual program that they had provided for twenty-two
years with a district-wide, structured English immersion program.
The stated goal of the program is to have all Limited-English Proficient (LEP) students become fluent in English in the shortest time
possible, so that they may achieve academic success in school. The
complete article appearing in *READ Perspectives* (Vol. V, No. 2) is a
progress report on the first four years of the English acquisition pro-

gram. An earlier evaluation of the first three years of the program may be found in the Spring 1997 issue of *READ Perspectives* (Vol. IV, No. 1). As the data demonstrate, limited-English students in the new program are achieving a higher measure of English language learning in a shorter time than was the case in the earlier, Spanish bilingual program.

Bethlehem is a city of approximately 75,000 with about 14,000 students in its school system. Minorities account for 30 percent of the student population: 24 percent are Hispanic, 5 percent are African-American, and 1 percent are Asian. About a quarter of the students in the school system come from economically disadvantaged backgrounds. The English Acquisition Program serves 1,400 limited-English students, approximately one child in ten within the school district.

Throughout its history, Bethlehem's English acquisition program has been receptive to community opinions. During an extensive planning phase, input was sought from parents, teachers, and students as well as from experts in the area of English language learning. In subsequent internal evaluations of the program, these same groups were surveyed for additional opinions and information. Parent surveys were printed in Spanish and English. As reported by the program office, 81 percent of the parents of students in the English Acquisition Program stated that their children had positive feelings about their school, while fully 88 percent responded that their child's work was appropriate for his or her grade level. Parents cited improvements for their children in spoken language, written language, independent reading, and in social interaction with peers.

One major change in the Bethlehem program was to eliminate busing of LEP students to special schools for Spanish bilingual instruction. Instead, these students are assigned to regular homerooms and classrooms in their neighborhood school as soon as they enter the district. Then, after evaluation for English language skills, they are placed in one of three program levels:

- *Beginner* level students understand little or no English;
- *Intermediate* level students understand spoken English, but require repetition and rephrasing; and
- *Advanced* level students understand most adult speech, with the exception of some complex grammatical structures and are ca-

Table 1

Longitudinal Data for Classes Entering in 1993-94 and 1994-95

English Language Acquisition Program	Class entering 1993–94 At the end of four years		Class entering 1994–95 At the end of three years	
Program Level	*Number*	*Percent*	*Number*	*Percent*
Already Exited	100	60	64	36
Advanced Level	30	18	48	27
Intermediate Level	28	17	51	29
Beginner Level	8	5	14	8
Total for the group	167	100	177	100
Special Education	13	21		
Total Students	180		198	

pable of doing regular classroom work in English with little or no special help.

To exit the program, a student must be able to participate successfully in a regular classroom with no further support from the English for Speakers of Other Languages (ESOL) program. At each school, a special team determines when a student is ready to exit. Students are monitored not only for spoken English development, but also for reading and writing skills.

In 1997, a school-to-work program for seriously at-risk, limited-English high school students was established in conjunction with St. Luke's Hospital. The goal of the program is to motivate these students to stay in school and to improve their English language skills and science knowledge, as well as to show them real career opportunities in the health care field. The first year results of this health career program illustrate its success: Sixteen low achieving limited-English students were enrolled; three moved out of the district; two did not complete the program; and of the eleven graduating seniors who did complete it, four were hired by the hospital.

Bethlehem reports the data in the following table as objective evidence of the success of the new English language program. Although the Bethlehem report is not a classic research study, because it lacks a control group, it is an accurate picture of student progress from year to year. Apart from special education students, 36 percent of LEP students in the class entering in 1994–95 had learned English so well that they exited from the program at the end of only three years. Another 27 percent had reached the advanced level. Thus, in total, 63 percent (nearly two-thirds) of students had advanced within three years to a level at which they were able to benefit fully from regular classroom instruction in English with minimal or no ESOL support. This success is even more dramatic after four years. As may be seen in Table 1, the data show that within four years, 60 percent of student participants had exited from the program, while another 18 percent were performing at the advanced level. For an interesting perspective on this remarkable success, consider that in California the re-designation rate for limited-English students to exit from bilingual programs was only 6.7 percent in 1997, and was reported to average 5 percent per year in the two previous years (Debra Camillo, California Department of Education).

Making a major change from a bilingual program to a program of structured English immersion requires determination, flexibility, planning, and a willingness to deal with details. Clearly, these conditions are present in Bethlehem. Bethlehem parents are very supportive of instruction in English and eager for their children to prepare for success in a largely English-speaking environment. Bethlehem's former bilingual instruction teachers received professional training in structured English strategies and are largely responsible for the consistency and documented success of the English acquisition program.

The evidence in Bethlehem demonstrates that children can and do learn English rapidly and effectively and that school subjects taught in English can be successfully mastered in a structured immersion program. In the Bethlehem schools, students of different language and cultural backgrounds can achieve academically in the regular school program after a relatively brief period of intensive special help. By providing limited-English students with educational opportunities equal to those of regular students, Bethlehem is firm in its belief that these students will be better prepared to participate in the full range of opportunities in the English-speaking community.

FROM PRIMARY LANGUAGE INSTRUCTION TO ENGLISH IMMERSION: HOW FIVE CALIFORNIA DISTRICTS MADE THE SWITCH

Kevin Clark

On its face, it seems simple enough: Teach immigrant students English through English. Put another way, stop teaching Limited-English Proficient (LEP) students through their primary language and use English. In its most absurd form, it was interpreted as 51 percent of the school day in English, 49 percent in Spanish. But no matter how the message was phrased, twisted, spindled or spun, it all boiled down to this: The day after California's voters passed the much-discussed Proposition 227, the loud, clear message was "teach English and do it quickly."

What followed after the passage of California's bellwether legislation requiring that immigrant school children be taught English in specially designed English immersion classrooms ranged from incredulity to celebration. During the months leading up to the vote, California was at the center of a national policy debate centered on how best to teach English to non-English speaking students. After twenty-two years of dubious results with state-imposed bilingual programs, educators, parents, and policymakers were asking why the state's 1.4 million LEP students were not learning English well or rapidly. A fractured and contentious debate had as its varied venues the local barbershop, the editorial page, and the school staff lounge. Everybody, it seemed, knew a little something about teaching English.

It is perhaps not surprising then that in the weeks and months after its passage those most immediately affected by the law's mandate—teachers, schools, districts, county offices, and the California Department of Education itself—quickly adopted one of four attitudes:

1. The law passed but will surely be overturned by the courts, the legislature, the "feds," the new governor, by someone, or some agency—so we'll wait.
2. Yes, it passed, but we will act as if it did not pass and do things as we always have.
3. It passed, so let's get on with implementing a legally compliant program.
4. This is what we have always wanted, so let's get to work.

Headlines, radio shows, local demonstrations, and staff lounge chat could all be easily slotted into one of the four response patterns. From San Francisco Superintendent Bill Rojas' public proclamation that he would go to jail before implementing the new law (Asimov, 1998), to organized attempts by Los Angeles Unified School District teachers and others to defy the law's requirement for English instruction (Elias, 1998; Moore, 1998), to silent, less publicized celebrations of common sense prevailing over ideology, the responses covered the spectrum. But in those weeks following the proposition's passage, the actions of California schools and districts that moved rapidly to implement structured English immersion programs would tell an even more dramatic story. This article recounts the events and experiences of five California school districts—from populous urban settings to small, isolated rural communities—that took a previously little understood concept of immersion language teaching and turned it into a successful reality. In their respective journeys to implementation, each was forced to confront many of the same issues, challenges, snags, and criticism. But in the end they all agreed that the transformation from bilingual approaches to English immersion education required a complete—and sometimes difficult and emotional—rethinking and re-conceptualization of how to educate today's Limited-English Proficient (LEP) students.

The first part of this article describes the five districts profiled throughout. The second part sets forth three significant issues that made planning for English immersion difficult. The third part sets forth some program implementation issues that surfaced in all of the districts and how they were resolved. The article concludes with a description of the common evaluation design used in all of the districts and presents some preliminary student achievement data.

THE CASE STUDY DISTRICTS

1. Orange Unified School District: Located in Southern California not too far from Disneyland, the Orange Unified School District enrolls nearly 28,000 students in grades K-12. Of these, more than 7,000 are Limited-English proficient. In 1997 the district petitioned the state board of education for a "waiver" of the requirement to hire additional bilingual teachers and to continue providing primary language instruction (mainly Spanish) in its bilingual education program. After months of acrimonious wrangling with the California Department of Education and legal bills in excess of $300,000, the district was granted permission to implement its *Structured English Immersion Program* in the fall of 1997, nearly nine months before passage of Proposition 227. Almost 5,500 elementary LEP students are enrolled in this program.

2. Delano Union Elementary School District: Enrolling nearly 6,100 students—3,000 of whom are LEP—in grades kindergarten through eight—the district is situated in California's agricultural heartland, between Bakersfield and Fresno. Headquarters for the Unified Farm Workers Union, the district has a long history of educating immigrant children through bilingual education programs. Its high proportion of LEP students put the district on the California Department of Education's yearly compliance monitoring list. The district eliminated all bilingual programs after Proposition 227 and implemented its *Sheltered English Immersion Program* for nearly 1,700 LEP students, featuring more than 90 immersion classrooms in fall 1998.

3. Atwater Elementary School District: Located 80 miles east of San Francisco, the district enrolls 4,500 students, one-third of whom are LEP. This K-8 district has operated for the past four years under an Office for Civil Rights (OCR) monitoring arrangement that called for increased primary language instruction, including the hiring of an additional 30 bilingual teachers in spite of mixed results in student achievement for bilingual instruction. After the passage of Proposition 227, the district dismantled its bilingual program and started its English immersion program, known locally as *Accelerated Classes for English*, in August 1998.

4. Ceres Unified School District: This central California K-12 district of 9,500 students features a relatively low percentage of LEP students at just under 10 percent. In prior years it had concentrated its bilingual staff at two or three of the district's 13 sites, including the high school. Ceres, too, eliminated its bilingual program and replaced it with the *Accelerated Language Academy* in the fall of 1998.

5. Riverdale Unified School District: This 1,329-student rural district, located one hour by car west of Fresno has one of the highest county percentages of LEP students at 38 percent. The district has three sites: two elementary schools and a comprehensive high school. In August 1997, the district, acting on demands from its parents and teachers, petitioned the State Board of Education for a waiver to eliminate bilingual instruction and to implement a K-12 immersion program. Neither the State Board of Education nor the Department of Education ever responded to that request. Ten months later, Proposition 227 passed. The district began its *High Intensity English Immersion Academy* in fall 1998.

GETTING ENGLISH IMMERSION STARTED: THREE SIGNIFICANT ISSUES

As these districts planned for implementation of their English immersion programs, each was faced by several common issues. This section delineates those issues and relates some possible causes for each.

Issue #1: Defining Terms

> *"Sheltered English immersion was not on any of the tests I took to become a teacher in this state. How can it be considered a 'real' program if no one taught it to us?"*—Kindergarten teacher

> *"Our bilingual program is really more like an immersion program, so as far as I'm concerned we can keep doing our bilingual program."*—Elementary school administrator

Few terms in public education are ever truly defined. In the field of language minority education it's a virtual minefield of semantic explosives. As Rossell (1998) has pointed out, there is little agreement over even basic terms. For example, what is a "bilingual" program? What is a "bilingual" teacher? What does "immersion" really mean? Is it the same as "submersion"? How about "sheltered" instruction? Do we even all agree on what "ESL" is—English as a Second Language (or ELD—English Language Development—as it is known in California)? This lack of term specifics spirals out of control at a school or district level, especially when a program change is in the offing. Can a school or district have bilingual "classes" without having a bilingual "program," or vice versa? Can you have a "sheltered" program for students who do not possess an intermediate set of English language skills? Is being taught *in* English the same as being taught English?

Bilingual Good—Immersion Bad

Whose definitions of terms were to be accepted? This question of semantics was indeed the first big issue facing districts that moved to implement English immersion. For California educators, many of the terms in the Proposition 227 law were virtually unknown or had negative connotations. Years of mandated teacher training following a prescribed, ideological syllabus had left teachers with the impression that "bilingual" education (in all its forms) was good, desirable, proven by research, better for kids, and endorsed by the only two linguists most had ever heard of—Steve Krashen and Jim Cummins [of the University of Southern California and the University of Toronto, respectively; both are leading advocates of bilingual education]. By contrast, most teacher training programs rarely referred to immersion, which was usually confused with "submersion" and therefore placed in the "bad" column as being anti-immigrant (does not affirm their home language), unrealistic in its expectations (rapid language learning) and denigrating to students' self-esteem (through ostensible loss of the home language). This view was further supported by California Department of Education policy and staff who over the years had pressured districts through compliance reviews, threats of funding interruptions, and mandated bilingual teacher training (Clark, 1998).

School administrators believed they should at least say they were trying to build a bilingual program, even if they did not believe it best for their students or found local difficulties to its implementation. Dr. Neil McKinnon, assistant superintendent of the Orange Unified School District and point person of the district's efforts to drop bilingual and implement an English immersion program, tangled repeatedly with California Department of Education officials. "They [department and compliance officials] believe in bilingual education," says McKinnon. "They were vested in it and thought it was the only way to go. Underlying that was an arrogance that they could make people do it how they wanted it done."

A popular misconception in all the districts was that "immersion" and "submersion" are synonymous. In the Delano Union Elementary School District, the perceived interchangeability of the two terms was initially problematic and added to the difficulty district educators had in understanding the new "Sheltered English Immersion" program. Kevin Monsma, director of special projects for the district and a former bilingual teacher, remembers the semantic issues well. "There were some teachers who saw our proposed English immersion program as submersion," Monsma says. "You really had to define the difference between the two before people understood what we wanted to do." English immersion programs require a special curriculum, texts, and trained teachers to provide English language instruction and subject matter at the same time—it is a program designed for English language learners. "Submersion" implies doing nothing special at all for limited-English students beyond placing them in a regular classroom and expecting them to learn the new language randomly. There is no comparison.

The Law's Language
The actual language of the law seemed only to fan the flames of semantic confusion. It called for an instructional program "not normally intended to exceed one year" that would be taught "overwhelmingly" in English and that would feature special "English language classrooms." These terms inspired doubt and confusion among educators when interpreted through the lens of what had been presented as gospel for years by the Department of Education and various institutions of higher education. It's little wonder so many educators protested. After all, educators had been assured, repeatedly, of the rightness of these premises: that Limited-English Proficient students need long periods (three to seven years) of primary language instruction; that English language learning usually takes

five, seven, or even ten years; that English instruction should be limited until primary language skills are fully developed. Proposition 227 now asked them to believe that English could be *taught* (and not just *acquired*), that there was indeed a program to accomplish such a goal (immersion), that students could gain significant English skills in one year, and that students could learn core school subjects presented in English.

Dr. Sandra Lenker, superintendent of the Atwater Elementary School District in Central California, points out that discarding old beliefs about language-minority education was both "liberating" and a bit worrisome. "The studies that had been presented to us over and over said that kids taught in their primary language did better over time," says Lenker. "These were national studies, and the people who presented them had the credentials. Still, in our heart of hearts, the immersion idea always made sense."

"English-Through-English"
Other terms that demanded local clarification were those aspects of the law mandating that classroom instruction be conducted "overwhelmingly" in English, and that LEP students receive "nearly all" of their instruction in English (English Language Education for Immigrant Children Initiative, Article 1, p. 2). At a policy level, district leaders were forced to take a stand—or not. Some districts left the amount of English instruction up to the teachers, effectively leaving open the option of continued primary language instruction (Terry, 1998). In the Atwater Elementary School District, the board of trustees adopted as part of their immersion plan specific instances in which the primary language of students would or could be used (see Chart 1). Another district used a percentage approach: "Ninety percent of the instruction will be in English." In Ceres Unified School District, the amount of English was the toughest issue of all. Most of the district's seven bilingual teachers (all Spanish speaking) were concentrated at one school which had previously had bilingual classes. At the district's other 12 schools, including a comprehensive high school, bilingual staff were few. Moreover, the district's LEP population was mixed: Spanish speakers were the majority, but there were Hmong, Lao, and Arabic speakers as well. Most of the immersion teachers knew only English. Spanish-speaking teachers demanded the right to use Spanish as part of their instruction. After

Chart 1 - Comparison of English Language Use Policies

SCHOOL DISTRICT	POLICY
Ceres Unified School District	The English language is to be used at all times during regular classroom instruction. Teachers and instructional paraprofessionals are not to use the child's primary language during any instructional activities. Students may use their home language during instruction, but should be encouraged to utilize English as much as possible. Emergency and health-related issues, playground interactions with peers and teachers, and communication with parents in a child's primary language is acceptable and encouraged.
Atwater Elementary School District	The predominant language of instruction in immersion classrooms is English. It should be the language of directions, instruction, discussion, and routine tasks. In those cases where a non-English language is utilized by the teacher or by an instructional assistant, it should meet one of the following criteria:

1.   Emergency communications related to safety and welfare of students.
2.   Clarification for a student, or group of students, of a word, concept, or idea.
3.   Explanation of directions or instructions pertinent to a specific task.
 4.   Communications with a parent, or legal guardian, of a student.

protracted debate, the district decided to adopt a 100 percent English language use policy for instructional purposes (see Chart 1). Dr. Marilyn Hildebrandt, assistant superintendent of instruction, recalls the difficult process of arriving at that decision. "We kept preaching the more English the better," she says. "If we had not made a major statement about language use, it would have dissipated the intent of immersion quickly."

Breaking Old Habits

At one California high school, use of Spanish by teachers and instructional assistants in English immersion classrooms was so prevalent the district adopted a guideline restricting Spanish use to no more than 90 consecutive seconds. Though perhaps comical at first glance, classroom observations had revealed that teachers were routinely utilizing Spanish for extended time periods in classrooms where English teaching was the goal. At one point, it became necessary at a staff meeting to use a watch to illustrate how much could be accomplished in 90 seconds, alleviating teachers' concerns that they needed more time to teach English by using Spanish. At a later meeting to review the district's English immersion program, a Department of Education consultant laughingly referred to the "typo" in the plan limiting primary language use to 90 seconds. He sat dumbfounded as district officials explained the need to clearly set language use guidelines for teachers who for years had used Spanish extensively, even in ESL classes.

In short, all of these districts had to come to terms with "terms." Though difficult, narrowing the meaning of terms in the formative part of the program spared needless grief and misunderstandings later. "I think we all finally agree on what we mean when we speak with one another," says Hildebrandt.

ISSUE #2: SO, WHAT IS IMMERSION?

> *"We've always had immersion. We've mixed our LEP students with English-only students for years."*—Elementary Resource Teacher

> *"Can we still listen to bilingual radio even though we have an English immersion program?"*—School Administrator

Chart 2 - A Comparison of Program Principles

ENGLISH IMMERSION	PRIMARY LANGUAGE/ BILINGUAL
Utilizes the English language for most instruction, and uses special strategies for teaching school subjects and second language simultaneously.	Students can learn best in their native language. Native language instruction ensures access to the core curriculum and grade promotion.
Features specialized groupings of English learners away from native speakers for one year only; common practice in bilingual programs is segregation for several years.	Segregation of students is bad. Sends a message of shame to non-English-speaking students that they have to be taught alone for some period of the day.
Maximizes the amount of understandable instruction in the new language.	English learning is dependent on the "transfer" of information learned through the primary language.
Seeks to accelerate English learning by increasing time spent learning English.	More primary language equals more English learning.
Instruction is geared to the students' developing English language level; English is actively "taught" using school subjects as the focus of the language lessons.	A good lesson will accelerate everyone's English, and they'll "acquire" all the language structures they need (past perfect subjunctive, reflexive pronoun use, etc.).
Success in learning a new language quickly creates confidence for future learning.	Primary language instruction is necessary to maintain and build students' self-esteem.

For all intents and purposes, the Orange Unified School District injected the word "immersion" into California's language-minority education debate when it petitioned the California State Board of Education for permission in mid-1997 to eliminate its bilingual programs and replace them with something it called "Structured English Immersion." During the Proposition 227 debate, immersion for some became synonymous with simply eliminating primary language instruction and replacing it with English language instruction. This interpretation brought numerous testimonials from talk radio junkies of their relatives' success with "sink-or-swim," and how they had "made it" with no special help. For other educators, immersion was associated with Canada and its success in teaching French to native English speakers, an approach more accurately described as "two-way immersion" or "dual immersion" (Genesee, 1984). As the debate intensified leading up to the June 2, 1998, vote on Proposition 227, opponents argued that "Sheltered English Immersion" (the term used in the law) was a "non-program," an "experiment" being pushed on California's LEP students, that it was "untested" and "untried" (Lelyveld, 1999). It would be more accurate to describe immersion education for many California educators, Department of Education officials, and pundits as unacknowledged, disallowed, and long-resisted.

It Wasn't on the Test
If the concept is a simple one, the confusion over what "immersion" really is can be at least partially attributed to the mass teacher training efforts in California that, clearly, have striven to undermine the presentation of second language teaching principles based on immersion. California educators over the years have been forced to take course work designed to prepare them to teach LEP students (Clark, 1998). Some form of test usually followed these training programs, the curriculum for which was approved by the state-level Commission on Teacher Credentialing. A review of this curriculum shows scant attention dedicated to informing California educators about immersion education, its history, where it is used, and its results. Instead, teachers are fed a steady diet of information that basically endorses native language instruction. Indeed, many non-bilingual educators emerged from these training programs probably more knowledgeable about bilingual programs (one in which they could not teach) than about English immersion, a program

design at least more consistent with most districts' and schools' resources (English-speaking teachers and English-language materials). Indeed, the principles of immersion education were almost dialectically opposed to what up until the passage of Proposition 227 had been considered absolute truth in some circles—the necessity for years of instruction through the primary language. Chart 2 presents a contrast between the principles of immersion and the "California primary language instruction model" to help illustrate the changes in thinking necessary for successful immersion program implementation.

Of course, charts are always easier to read than to implement. As each of these districts began discussing the immersion concept, it was typical for people to argue—sometimes very passionately—about the need for continued primary language instruction. One key question that seemed to focus attention was a simple one: Are our students becoming English proficient in our current program? The answer to this question was usually "no." "It came down to the

Chart 3 - English Immersion Program
Placement Criteria, Elementary

Entry Criteria	Program	Goal	Exit Criteria
Pre-production	Sheltered Immersion	English Development	
Early Production	Sheltered Immersion	English Development	IntermediateFluency Grade-Appropriate
		Literacy Skills	
Speech Emergent	Sheltered Immersion	English Development	
Int. FluentSDAIE	Academic	Achievement / Core Curriculum	
Adv. Fluent SDAIE/ Mainstream/ Achievement	Academic	Redesignation toFEP Core Curriculum	
Fluent English	Proficient Mainstream	Academic Achievement	Graduation / Proficiencies

Chart 4 - Dual Selection Criteria for Secondary LEP Students

Low Oral English, Low English Literacy	Sheltered English Immersion	English Development Listening Speaking Reading Writing	Int. Fluency Grade appropriate Literacy skills
Intermediate Oral English, Low English Literacy	Sheltered English Immersion	English Development Content Area Reading Content Area Writing	Grade appropriate Literacy skills

progress—or lack of progress—that our LEP students were making in our previous bilingual classrooms," recalls James Brooks, superintendent of Riverdale Unified School District. "What we were doing was very inadequate." Dr. Sandra Lenker, superintendent of Atwater Elementary School District agrees. "Across the grades we had little accurate information about how our students were progressing in English," she says. "I still remember our realization that most of our LEP students were only receiving 30 minutes a day of ELD instruction. It was an 'a ha' for all of us. How could you learn English in just 30 minutes a day?"

Still, letting go of primary language instruction—though generally acknowledged to be an ineffective approach in these districts—became easier as teachers internalized the principles of immersion language teaching. Dr. Neil McKinnon, Orange Unified's assistant superintendent, recalls that once the immersion idea was explained and removed from the emotional arena, educators across the district quickly realized that this was a program the district could actually do. "Immersion turned out to be the most coherent program we have ever offered LEP students," says McKinnon. "Prior to that, LEP students were seen as the bilingual teachers' responsibility and one that the majority of teachers didn't have to worry about. The immersion program changed that attitude completely."

ISSUE #3: DESIGNING THE PROGRAM

"Shouldn't we wait until they tell us how to do immersion?"
—Elementary School Principal

"It seems pretty clear to me that we use English to teach them English. That's the program!"—Elementary School Teacher

Having defined terms and gained an understanding of immersion education, each of the districts moved aggressively into designing the actual program. Dr. Marilyn Hildebrandt, of Ceres Unified School District, recalls that it felt like "re-inventing" the whole school district. "We were designing a program that none of us had ever really seen in California," she says. "We soon realized that everything we did with immersion was going to touch some other aspect of the district, from transportation to report cards to teacher training." What follows is a detailed review of the immersion program designs adopted by these districts, showing how their programs responded to five basic immersion questions:

Which students will be included in our immersion program?
Proposition 227 called for districts to design a sheltered English immersion program that would develop in students a "good working knowledge" of English. To arrive at their definition of this term, the districts worked backward. If intermediate level students were candidates for modified, grade-appropriate content (known as Specially Designed Academic Instruction in English, or SDAIE), then "good working knowledge" could be called intermediate fluency. These students would possess grade-appropriate English skills in oral comprehension and speaking, with reading and writing skills approaching that level. Logically, then, students with less than intermediate skills (less than a good working knowledge) would be candidates for immersion. It became immediately clear, however, that not all LEP students fall into such a neat sorting arrangement. Indeed, older students tended to demonstrate two very different profiles: Some spoke English with almost native speaker fluency, but their reading and writing skills in English were at the second- or third-grade level. Another group lacked both oral English *and* English literacy skills. Thus was born a bifurcated criteria for immersion program placement for older students (grades 7 through 12). Charts 3 and 4 show

an immersion placement grid, including the "dual criteria" for older LEP students.

> *Note:* At the secondary level, each of these immersion cohorts received a different program; those with low English oral (speaking skills) and low English literacy skills (reading and writing) received a program that addressed all those areas, while the students who lacked only English literacy skills took courses like "Content Area Reading Strategies" and "Writing in the Content Areas" to address their specific English literacy needs.

Once the placement criteria had been defined, most of the districts realized that their current knowledge of their students' English proficiency was poor, incomplete, or outdated. Because most districts utilize the state-mandated English proficiency tests more for compliance purposes than for program placement, several of the districts found themselves without up-to-date, useable placement data. It was common in all of the districts for many students—in some cases hundreds—to be re-tested to obtain a valid and current measure. One district scurried to train their 38 immersion program teachers in how to determine English fluency levels by administering the Student Oral Language Observation Matrix (SOLOM) "For really the first time perhaps in our district's history," recalls one site principal, "we actually have accurate assessment data on these students that we use for program placement and instruction."

For how much of the school day will students be in an immersion classroom?
The next issue faced by schools and districts in designing an immersion program was to decide what would characterize an immersion classroom and how much time per day students would spend there learning English. Both issues presented problems. First, the law clearly made a distinction between an "English language classroom" and an "English language mainstream classroom." The implication was startling to some: Should we create classrooms composed solely of English learners of less than intermediate fluency? Again, the rationale was tangled with old ideas of language learning and their definitions. Some teachers in all districts quickly challenged the idea of segregating these students for their English instruction. "Put them in regular classes," they rallied, not understanding that they were calling for "submersion," a program in which English learners

are mixed with native speakers and expected to master English and core content at a level designed for native speakers—with no special help.

Other teachers quickly supported the clustering idea, drawing perhaps unknowingly on several principles of immersion language education. First, putting the limited-English students together allows a teacher to design specific English language lessons suited to their needs. Second, by removing native English speakers, a teacher could more effectively provide comprehensible subject matter instruction using English. Lastly, time on task—learning English—could be intensified by the formation of these special classrooms. "It made such perfect sense," says one second-grade teacher. "I saw then that English could be taught very quickly because the students were all learning the same thing—English."

For each of the districts, the decision to form immersion classrooms comprised solely of English learners was controversial since it went against the notion that homogeneity in student groupings was to be avoided (unless, of course, it was a bilingual program). In Orange Unified, with twenty-eight elementary schools featuring LEP student concentrations ranging from five at one elementary school to more than 850 at another, the issue was resolved by adopting three different grouping models, depending on the number of LEP students at a site. At those schools with high concentrations (more than 40 percent LEP), LEP students stayed together for most of the day, since many of the classrooms already featured a majority of LEP students. Mid-size schools adopted a clustering model, where for a certain part of the day LEP students were grouped by fluency stage for English instruction. Schools with LEP concentrations of less than 10 percent also clustered, which sometimes meant mixing several grades together for English language instruction. In Atwater, with seven elementary sites, it was relatively easy to cluster LEP students into immersion classes. The biggest challenge was at grades 4, 5 and 6, which each had fewer than seven immersion candidates. They were eventually pooled into one classroom. In Riverdale, the numbers were just about right for one class per grade, with the exception of the secondary grades, which were clustered into a seven-eight mix and a nine-twelve mix.

Chart 6

Elementary or Self-contained

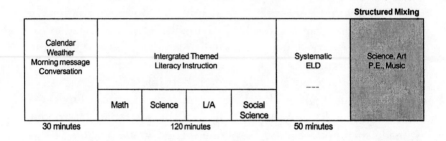

						Structured Mixing
Calendar Weather Morning message Conversation	Intergrated Themed Literacy Instruction				Systematic ELD	Science, Art P.E., Music
	Math	Science	L/A	Social Science	---	
30 minutes	120 minutes				50 minutes	

Secondary - Low Oral English, Low English Literacy

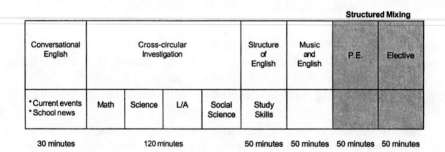

							Structured Mixing	
Conversational English	Cross-circular Investigation				Structure of English	Music and English	P.E.	Elective
*Current events *School news	Math	Science	L/A	Social Science	Study Skills			
30 minutes	120 minutes				50 minutes	50 minutes	50 minutes	50 minutes

Secondary - Intermediate Oral English, Low English Literacy

High Intensity Literacy Development

Content area Reading strategies	Content area Writing	Study Skills	Science (SDAIE)	Math (SDAIE or Mainstream)	P.E.	Elective
50 minutes	50 minutes	50 minutes	50 minutes	50 minutes	50 minutes	50 minutes

How much of each day's instructional time will be in English?
If time-on-task is a central tenet of immersion theory, then more time spent learning English should result in more English learned. At an implementation level it boils down to this: How much time will students spend learning English—*and learning in English*—each day? California newspapers covered this issue extensively after Proposition 227 passed. Advocates of primary language instruction argued that 51 percent of the day was all the law required in the way of English instruction; the other 49 percent could be spent in the primary language (DeFao, 1998). In one particularly bizarre twist, anti-immersion educators buzzed over a California Association for Bilingual Education (CABE) bulletin outlining the pro-bilingual group's interpretation of "overwhelmingly in English" (CABE, 1998). In that bulletin it stated that since a judge's ruling on the legality of Proposition 227 had referred to the "overwhelming" 61 percent of votes in favor of the initiative, that meant that a student had only to spend 61 percent of the instructional day learning English, freeing up 39 percent of the day for primary language instruction. All the districts described here rejected these nonsensical interpretations and turned to writings on European immersion programs for guidance. District officials found that indeed most or all of the instruction during an immersion student's day was in the target language (Glenn, 1996). If the home language was utilized, it was used primarily for short-term explanations or was offered as an after-school option. Only Orange Unified included in its plan an allowance for up to 30 minutes per day of formalized home language assistance. This use of the home language was limited to students of pre-production or early production fluency stages. Moreover, this type of instruction—in most cases provided by an instructional assistant—followed a strict set of guidelines, including specific methods and activities.

Structured Mixing
Finally, all of the profiled districts agreed that immersion students should spend some part of their day learning together with native-English speaking students during a time that came to be called "structured mixing." During this time, immersion students would be mixed together with fluent English proficient students to engage in tasks like hands-on science, art, music, or drama. The rationale was simple: Immersion students need to practice their developing English lan-

guage skills with other English speakers. Several residual benefits of mixing were quickly identified. First, the mixing time gave immersion teachers at least a short break during the day. "Language teaching is very rewarding, but it is also very tiring," said one teacher at a district immersion meeting. The mixing time also sent a strong message to all district teachers that LEP students were still everyone's responsibility—not just the immersion teachers'. Kevin Monsma of Delano looks at the structured mixing time as one of the most valuable components of the district's immersion program. "Once we worked out the logistics, structured mixing has become one of the most important times of the day for immersion students since they are using their English and working with other English-speaking students during that time," says Monsma.

Not surprisingly, all of the districts profiled here adopted program designs of a similar nature. Chart 5 shows a graphic rendering of the three basic components to all of the immersion programs, followed by a short description of each component.

Chart 5

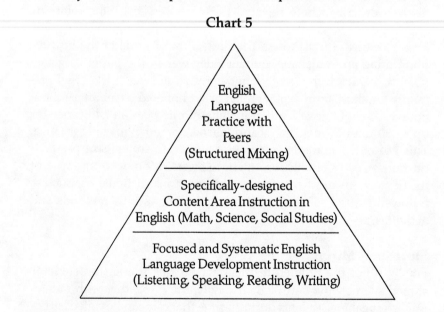

KEY COMPONENTS

1. <u>Focused and Systematic English Language Development (ELD)</u>: Each immersion student receives a comprehensive

program of ELD daily, which is provided by a credentialed teacher. This instruction focuses on all aspects of the English language (listening, speaking, reading, and writing) and utilizes the district's adopted ELD materials.

2. Modified, Comprehensible Core Instruction: All immersion students participate as fully as possible in the district's regular core program through the provision of modified instruction, known as Specially Designed Academic Instruction in English (SDAIE), provided by a credentialed teacher. Some of this content may be significantly modified to adapt it to the English capabilities of the learner.

3. Structured Mixing: All immersion students spend up to 75 minutes daily (this varies by district) learning together with non-LEP students. During this "mixing" time, students participate in varied activities, from science and art to music and drama. The purpose of this time is for immersion students to use their developing English skills with native English-speaking peers.

4. Design of the Instructional Day: Recognizing that variance in the instructional program could threaten implementation efforts and results, all of the districts profiled in this article crafted a daily schedule for immersion classrooms. Though prescriptive, the daily schedules turned out to be helpful for teachers as they planned daily tasks for immersion students. Moreover, the specific time allotments allowed the districts to show clearly the increased importance that English language teaching would have in the immersion program. To further support teachers in their understanding of the daily schedule, Delano Union Elementary School District produced an instructional video that led teachers through the minutes of the day. The video not only explained the immersion program, but featured actual lessons from district teachers and showed how these lessons related to the program's goals, principles, and intended outcomes. Chart 6 provides examples of daily schedules for both elementary and secondary immersion classrooms.

5. The Role of Content and Selection of Materials: Even for the most skilled teachers, the mandate to "teach English" was sometimes perplexing. Teachers would ask: Does this mean teaching all day the skills of English, i.e., nouns, verbs, direct

objects, and reflexive pronouns? Do I still teach social studies, math, and science? Do immersion students still have to
read the grade-level literature books? How do I teach reading? These and countless other questions were asked in all
the districts before and well into program implementation.
Complicating the issue was a steady barrage of press coverage quoting immersion foes and bilingual advocates who
said that immersion students would fall woefully behind, be
bored to tears by hour after hour of English sentence dia-
gramming, and that their self-esteem would be crushed by
instruction in a foreign language. In a particularly bizarre
twist, the Los Angeles Unified School District directed its
immersion teachers to withhold English reading lessons
(Colvin, 1998), apparently seeking to "alleviate" some of these
forecasted outcomes.

The five districts studied here adopted a much more rea-
soned approach. "We told our teachers that the primary goal of the
immersion program was to teach English skills in listening, speaking, reading, and writing," says Dr. Hildebrandt of Ceres Unified.
"But we also told them that in many cases content areas would be
the vehicle, i.e., the 'subject,' of these lessons." In Orange Unified,
the district offered an ongoing series of practical, hands-on work-
shops that showed teachers how to use content-area subjects for
language development. A lesson on the life cycle, for example, was
a good time to teach words related to trees, seeds, and spring. "The
Little Red Hen" provided a nice forum for expanding students' range
of adjectives for describing people. Bobbi Ochoa, Orange Unified's
immersion program resource teacher, remembers that teachers had
to learn to look at subject matter as both academic content and as
English learning. "It wasn't hard for them to do this," she explains.
"It was just a new way of looking at things."

MOVING TO IMPLEMENTATION

As each of the districts neared the date to implement, it became
apparent that many of the same issues that had confronted the planning teams (semantics, lack of understanding of immersion, etc.)
would probably present themselves again in new forums. Though

each district's community was vastly different, there was much commonality in their approaches to these issues, each of which is explained below.

Parent Education
Notwithstanding evidence that a majority of immigrant parents support the teaching of English in public schools (Center for Equal Opportunity, 1996), the scene was sometimes less clear at a local level. Orange Unified, for example, had received ample press coverage because of parent opposition to its efforts to implement an immersion program in fall 1997. At the other extreme, Hispanic parents in the small rural town of Riverdale eagerly signed their names in the months prior to the vote on Proposition 227 to a district request to eliminate bilingual education and begin an immersion English program in grades K-12.

Table 1
Orange Unified School District

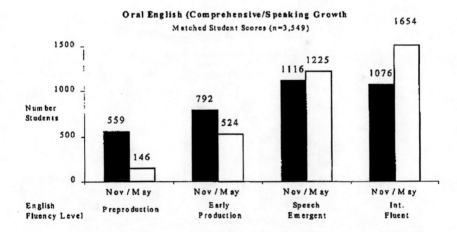

Oral English (Comprehensive/Speaking Growth
Matched Student Scores (n=3,549)

Survival Analysis				
Number Moved	Preproduction	Early Production	Speech Emergent	Int Fluent
% who moved from eligible	413	681	572	6
	74%	57%	32%	1%

Table 2
Atwater Elementary School District

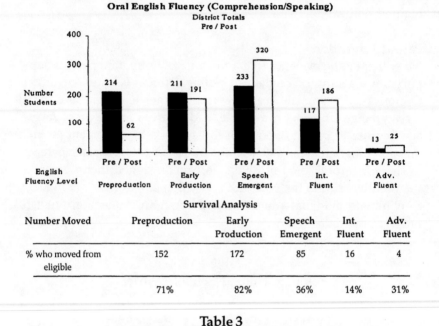

Oral English Fluency (Comprehension/Speaking)
District Totals
Pre / Post

Survival Analysis

Number Moved	Preproduction	Early Production	Speech Emergent	Int. Fluent	Adv. Fluent
% who moved from eligible	152	172	85	16	4
	71%	82%	36%	14%	31%

Table 3
Delano Unified School District

DUSD Oral English Protocol (Listening/Speaking)
Pre /Post
All Students (n=1,604)

Survival Analysis

Number Moved	Preproduction	Early Production	Speech Emergent	Int. Fluent	Adv. Fluent
% who moved from eligible	270	268	169	44	44
	49%	66%	40%	24%	100%

Adding to local moods was a much-discussed and little-understood provision of Proposition 227 that allowed parents to request an "alternative" program to the mandated English immersion design. Perhaps not surprisingly, reaction across the districts to the announcement that English immersion would be the predominant program was mixed. The central challenge where there was dissent was to educate parents—as the districts had done with staff—about what immersion is. Many parents, explains Dr. McKinnon of Orange, thought that immersion would leave their children with no special services. "We learned that it was very important to define the program in terms parents could understand," says McKinnon. "We had to communicate the program to the parents and let them know that we were going to take care of their kids."

Chart 7

Orange Unified School District
Relationship Between Oral English Fluency Stages and
Reading, Language and Mathematics Achievement
SAT9 Standardized Test, Spring 1998
Mean Scaled Scores (n=3,120)

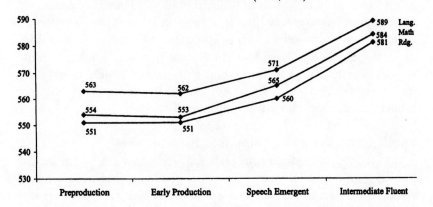

In Delano, Kevin Monsma braced for a round of parent meetings at each of the district's seven elementary schools, not knowing what to expect in an area that had featured bilingual programs for years. Despite some limited resistance, Monsma learned that the best spokespeople for the new program were district parents themselves. "The emotional aspects of the law initially clouded the need for information," he says. "We found that parents who believed in the

Chart 8

Atwater Elementary School District
Relationship Between Oral English Fluency Stage and
Reading Achievement After 90 Days of Instruction

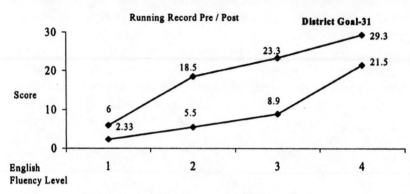

(Note: A score of 31 is considered on grade level)

idea were very persuasive to parents who were unsure or against it. We also encouraged them to come and visit the classrooms. It was a very open process, which in the end made things much easier." In Atwater, the reaction was similar. "We found that some parents who initially were opposed to immersion came to support it once they understood it better," says Superintendent Lenker. "We kept seeing very clearly that this was more than a program; to them it was their children." Waiver requests to get out of the immersion program totaled fewer than 50 between all five districts.

Public Relations and Community Perception

Soon after implementation in Delano, Kevin Monsma went on the public relations offensive. "We were proud of this program and were very open to discussion or comment," he says. Two weeks after school started, Monsma invited several media reporters to tour the schools and talk with teachers. The subsequent media profiles of the program were upbeat and positive, stressing how the district had used Proposition 227 as a mechanism for improving education for Limited-English Proficient students (Shrider, 1998; Schettler, 1998). In Atwater, the decision to call the new immersion program Accelerated Classes for English was part of a district effort to remove negative post-227 connotations from immersion and instead associate it with success, intensity, and purpose. Riverdale's High Intensity English Immersion Academy quickly established itself as a fast-track English learning program, where students were rewarded regularly at festive community gatherings with bronze, silver, or gold eagle lapel pins to demonstrate their increasing mastery of English.

In Orange, where the program had taken some hits in the media, positive anecdotal observations from teachers, parents, and administrators about students' success in learning English were bolstered by a mid-term progress report showing that 81 percent of immersion students had advanced to speech-emergent or intermediate English fluency. A front-page piece in the *Los Angeles Times* described the district program and offered a balanced profile of its successes and challenges (Anderson, 1998). Publication and distribution of tri-fold brochures written in a colloquial question-and-answer format also proved helpful to parents and community members trying to get a handle on the new program.

Leadership and Decisiveness
Unlike Orange and Riverdale, the other three districts had not thought through immersion education in any significant way prior to the public vote. Once Proposition 227 passed on June 2, 1998, districts had only 60 days to prepare for its implementation. "We all had a real lack of foresight as to the impact of what this law was going to do," recalls Lenker of Atwater. "Most of us probably thought it wouldn't pass because bilingual programs were so institutionalized in California," Dr. Hildebrandt of Ceres agrees. "We were in such a state of denial all summer," she says. "We all thought it was going to be overturned. Boy, were we wrong."

Once passed, though, the time line was short. Whereas Orange Unified and Riverdale Unified had crafted immersion plans and begun a dialogue in their districts nearly a year earlier, Ceres, Atwater, and Delano were caught flat-footed. To move quickly, each of the districts established a small working group that included direct participation of superintendents, assistant superintendents, key school principals, and the local school boards. In retrospect, Lenker credits her four-person planning group with the district's success in having a program in place at the starting gun. "This is not the kind of issue that you form 100 committees to decide," she says. "It's too emotional. We made a decision at an executive level, kept the board informed, and did it quickly."

In Ceres, the team met late into the evening and on a weekend; after five days, the plan was in draft form and ready for comment. The following week, it was presented to a group of teachers who had been selected to teach in the district's newly christened Accelerated Language Academy. Questions were asked, some tears were shed, and a few minor changes were made. Classes began the following week. Delano followed a similar time line and process: "We made a transition from bilingual education to immersion education in six weeks," says Monsma. "We took a few hits along the way, but the program is in place now and doing well."

Measuring Student Progress

As in many parts of the country, California public education is facing increased demands for accountability. There is some documentation showing that schools and districts have struggled in their efforts to collect clean, complete data on their LEP students' English learning progress. Though teachers can easily recount stories of rapid English learning and academic success (Sahagun, 1999), the quantitative back-up data are sometimes sorely missing. For that reason, each of the districts profiled here recognized the need for a rigorous, ongoing evaluation process for their structured English immersion programs. In a rare act of educational congruity, all of the districts independently decided on an evaluation design that the Orange Unified School District had utilized. By using the same design, the districts would be able to compare their data not only in house, but with the other districts.

The Orange Unified School District's evaluation featured two interesting approaches to measure the success of their immersion program. First, they adopted a statistical technique known as "survival analysis" to more accurately show LEP students' progress through the English oral fluency stages (preproduction, early production, speech emergent, intermediate fluency and advanced fluency). By examining the proportion of those who succeed in moving during a given time period, survival analysis calculates the rate at which children, among all of those who have an opportunity, move from one language learning stage to another. In this way, the districts can determine how long it takes students to move through the stages and can at any given time show how many students had exited a given fluency stage. This breakdown of the term "LEP" encourages teachers to be more aware of student movement through the fluency stages and how these stages can and should be used for instructional planning and grouping within a classroom.

Orange Unified's student data for English speaking and oral comprehension after the first year of immersion education is presented in Table 1 below. This information comes from district teachers who use a special English protocol to measure and record students' oral English development at three times during the year. Tables 2 and 3 show preliminary data for Atwater and Delano at the mid-point of their first year of immersion education using the same assessment instrument. Below each table is the survival analysis.

Reading and Writing Assessment

With respect to achievement in English reading and writing, the districts employ a "proficiency-matched" analysis that allows them to see the relationship between English oral fluency and literacy development, mathematics, or any other area (two of the districts also collect running records for reading achievement and rubric-scored writing assessments, each of which are matched to the oral fluency stage). This analysis is intended to explore a central tenet of immersion: that by accelerating English ability, students will more quickly be able to access the full range of the district's core curriculum. Charts 7 and 8 that follow show how proficiency-matched student achievement analysis is used for reporting standardized test data, and other reading and writing test data.

By using this evaluation design all of the districts established a systematic way of exploring in detail the full range of English development of their immersion students. Teachers, for their part, use the information to see which aspects of their instruction are yielding the most results. For example, in the Ceres Unified School District teachers' review and analysis of the program-wide data revealed that in the early part of the program there had been an emphasis placed on oral language development and a corresponding under-emphasis on writing development. This showed up in rapid oral language growth scores, but a generally lower growth rate in writing development. The data helped teachers to adjust the amount of time they spend each day teaching writing and also was the catalyst for important discussions about the actual writing tasks that immersion students were being asked to do. In short, by moving away from "LEP" data to a more complete language profile of immersion students, all of the districts were able to more successfully unify data collection and analysis with instructional improvement.

Conclusion

The passage of Proposition 227 in California sent a major shock wave through a state that had followed 22 years of bilingual ideology in spite of mixed results and varied factors that made it impossible for many districts to competently implement. The five districts profiled here had either already begun immersion education or quickly moved to do so after the passage of Proposition 227 in June 1998. Though very different in terms of size, location, and demographics, all of the districts encountered many of the same issues and challenges as they geared up for implementing English immersion and its subsequent day-to-day operation. This article suggests that as districts move away from primary language instruction, they are likely to find that undefined educational terminology, long-standing bilingual ideology, and poor understanding of what immersion is can make the initial going rough. Once implemented, districts and schools must make their program clear to parents and the community. Finally, well-designed evaluation plans and careful, consistent monitoring are imperative to show that the programs are accomplishing their goals.

References

Anderson, N. (1998). Pioneering district fuels bilingual education debate. *Los Angeles Times*, May 6, p.1.

Asimov, N. (1998). Educators working around prop. 227. *San Francisco Chronicle*, July 31, p. 1.

Center for Equal Opportunity. (1996). The importance of learning English: A national opinion survey of hispanic parents, August. Washington, D.C.

Clark, K. (1998). Declaration in the case of *Valeria G., et al. v. Pete Wilson, et al.*, July 15, 1998.

Colvin, R.L. (1998). Prop. 227 delays reading lessons in English in L.A. *Los Angeles Times*, Oct. 9, p. 1.

Crawford, J. (1999). *Bilingual education: History, politics, theory and practice.* Los Angeles: Bilingual Educational Services.

DeFao, J. (1998). School districts far apart on prop. 227. *Sacramento Bee*, Dec. 6, p. 1.

Elias, T. (1998). California teachers to defy bilingual ban. *Washington Times*, July 13, p.1.

Genesee, F. (1984). French immersion programs. In S. Shapson and V. D'Oyley (eds), *Bilingual and multicultural education: Canadian perspectives* (pp. 33–54). Clevedon, England: Multilingual Matters.

Glenn, C. (1996). *Educating immigrant children: Schools and language minorities in twelve nations.* NewYork: Garland Publishing.

Lelyveld, N. (1999). How anti-bilingual law translates in the class. *Philadelphia Inquirer*, March 11, p. 1.

Moore, S. (1999). Bilingual betrayal. *National Review*, Oct. 12, p. 23.

Rossell, C. (1998). Mystery on the bilingual express: A critique of the Thomas and Collier study,"School effectiveness for language minority students." *READ Perspectives*, 5 (2): pp. 5–32.

Schettler, B. (1998). District drafts immersion program. *Delano Record*, Aug. 6, p.1.

Shrider, M. (1998). Delano's English plan receives high marks. *The Bakersfield Californian*, Aug. 7, B1.

Terry, D. (1998). California bilingual teaching lives on after vote to kill it. *New York Times*, Oct. 3, p. 1.

ABOUT THE AUTHORS

DIANE AUGUST, a senior Program Officer at the National Research Council, is co-editor of the 1997 report, *Improving Schooling for Language-Minority Children: A Research Agenda*. In addition to her experience as a schoolteacher and school administrator in California, she has worked on education policy issues, school improvement and program evaluation, at the state and federal level.

MARIA ESTELA BRISK, a native of Argentina, is an Associate Professor and coordinator of the Bilingual Education Program at the School of Education, Boston University. Her professional interests include bilingual literacy acquisition and methodology of teaching reading and writing. She was the 1991 recipient of the Metcalf Cup and Prize for excellence in teaching at Boston University. She recently published *Bilingual Education: From Compensatory to Quality Schooling*.

MARY T. CAZABON has been involved in bilingual education for more than 20 years, including work in France, Spain and in the Cambridge, Massachusetts, Public Schools. She has concentrated on the development of two-way bilingual programs, and she is currently a doctoral candidate in the Leadership in Urban Studies Program at the University of Massachusetts, Boston.

KEVIN CLARK is a consultant and teacher educator specializing in instructional strategies for language minority students. He has advised more than one hundred school districts across the United States on the design, implementation, and evaluation of effective educational programs for second language learners.

EUGENE CREEDON has been the superintendent of the Quincy Public Schools since 1992. He has spent his professional career in the Quincy schools and has accumulated long years of experience administering programs for a multicultural/multilingual student body. His interests include minority student achievement and the second language learning process.

THOMAS J. DOLUISIO, superintendent of the Bethlehem Area School District in Pennsylvania since 1986, was educated at Pennsylvania State University and Lehigh University. He has been a high school science teacher, school principal, and superintendent in Bethlehem. His professional, long-standing interests include the development of effective programs for limited-English students and the full integration of these students in mainstream school and community life.

RICHARD M. ESTRADA has written for the *Dallas Morning News* since 1988 and since 1992 has been Associate Editor of the Editorial Page. He also writes a column syndicated by the Washington Post Writers Group. A native of New Mexico, Mr. Estrada is fluent in English and Spanish. He has traveled widely in Central and South America and the Caribbean as a journalist. Most recently, Mr. Estrada was honored by the National Alliance for the Mentally Ill which bestowed on him its 1998 award for writing on mental health issues. He served from 1992 through 1997 on the bipartisan U.S. Commission on Immigration Reform.

CHARLES L. GLENN is professor and chairman of Administration, Training and Policy Studies at Boston University. From 1970 to 1991 he directed urban education and equity efforts for the Massachusetts Department of Education. Glenn has authored hundreds of articles, books and monographs. His most recent book is *Educating Immigrant Children: Schools and Language Minorities in Twelve Nations* (1996).

HAROLD LANE, representative from the First Worcester District since 1993, is House Chairman of the Joint Committee on Education, Arts and Humanities in the Massachusetts Legislature. His professional experience includes teaching history at the secondary school level, serving as principal of Wachusett Regional High School from 1984-93 and as president of the Massachusetts Secondary School Administrators' Association in 1991-92. Representative Lane is a leader in promoting education reforms and improvements in Massachusetts.

MARK HUGO LOPEZ is an Assistant Professor at the University of Maryland's School of Public Affairs. He received his Ph.D. in Economics from Princeton University in 1996. He specializes in labor economics, the economics of education, and econometrics. His research has focused on long-term effects of bilingual education and vocational education on student achievement.

ROSALIE PEDALINO PORTER is the author of *Forked Tongue: The Politics of Bilingual Education* (1990, 1995), numerous articles and book chapters on the issues of second language teaching and learning, and effective programs for language minority students. She has lectured widely in the U.S., Europe, and Asia on education policy for immigrant, migrant, and refugee children.

CHRISTINE H. ROSSELL is professor of political science at Boston University. Her research interests and publications include school desegregation, bilingual education, and education policy. She has written four books, most recently *The Emperor Has No Clothes: Bilingual Education in Massachusetts*, published by the Pioneer Institute in Boston.

DOUGLAS SEARS is currently superintendent of the Chelsea Public Schools. Formerly he served as Assistant to the President of Boston University, and was chairman of the Boston Management Team which oversees the operations of the Chelsea school system. Before coming to Boston, Dr. Sears was a Foreign Service Officer in the American Embassies in Switzerland and the Philippines.

READ <small>The Institute for Research in English Acquisition and Development</small>

Previously in READ PERSPECTIVES:

READ Perspectives

is now an annual serial publication. Each issue will focus

on a theme of importance in the education of limited-English

students in U.S. public schools.

CALL FOR MANUSCRIPTS:

Volume VII, Fall 2000, will focus on the theme

ACCOUNTABILITY FOR BILINGUAL STUDENTS.

We are interested in articles on student achievement in schools and
districts;

reports on statewide testing systems; efforts to help English

language learners meet higher standards; promising new

program initiatives; effects of Proposition 227 on students'

second-language learning and academic progress.

Deadline for manuscripts: January 15, 2000

Length of articles and honoraria are negotiable.

Send proposals to:

The Editor, *READ Perspectives*,
815 15th Street N.W., Suite 930 • Washington, D.C. 20005